BUILD YOUR HOUSE

GW00734307

A GUIDE THAT WILL HAND YOU THE KEYS TO SELF-BUILD SUCCESS

BY

ANDY PATMORE

WEBSITE
www.buildyourownhouse.biz

PATMORE
PUBLISHING

Edition One.
2014

With special thanks to
Lisa Read
Karina Read
John Pagan

Disclaimer:
This book is intended to be used as a general guide; neither the author nor the publisher will
accept any responsibilities for any inaccuracies contained within this book. No one should act
on information contained within this book without first seeking professional advice. It must
be noted that due to the nature of the construction industry planning, legislation,
methodology and materials are constantly changing.

What is the aim of this book?

The aim is to provide the reader with the required information and advice on how to self-manage the building of your own home in the same manner as the professionals. It is not intended as a technical publication but to be used as a guide to enable you to have the required information needed while constructing your own dwelling.

Am I qualified?

I have been involved in the construction industry for over 30 years, spending much of my time dedicated to house building.

My house building experiences have been extensive and these include:-

Speculatively building single and multiple dwellings

Project Managing dwellings for private clients

Managing vast housing projects for national house builders

I have constructed many dwellings and other structures across the UK giving me a clear understanding of varying ground conditions and materials which are sometimes unique to the locality.

It would be impossible to write a book covering every aspect of constructing a house, from the initial concept to moving in. It would also be impossible to personally carry out the entire task yourself. So the aim has to be, how best you can manage your own project.

There's a fairly rigid procedure that needs to be followed as it would be foolhardy to choose your bathroom tiles before you have had your plans approved. A lot of what has been written here is based on pure common sense.

This book is also written in the same sequence as you would build your house project: step-by-step, phase by phase.

Keynotes
Important info will be highlighted as 'post it' notes. Don't cut corners on your self-build project. Knowledge is power!

I have set the book out in sequence, from the initial concept of your project to moving in. Depending on where you are up to with your project you may wish to skip some of the chapters.

It is worth noting that you can apply the following principal not only with the construction of a new dwelling, but also to an extension or even a refurbishment project.

I have tried where possible to write in layman's terms. Where this has not been possible, I have explained the meanings of certain words and phrases. It would be useful for you to try and remember expressions and terminology that are used in the construction industry as this will be of great benefit to you when negotiating various aspects of your project with industry professionals.

A.Patmore

Contents

1. You And Your Project — 9

2. Planning — 14

3. The Cost Of Your Project — 20

4. Finance — 26

5. Building Regulations — 30

6. Code For Sustainable Homes — 37

7. Warranties — 43

8. Budget — 46

9. Incoming Services — 50

10. Materials — 60

11. Producing A Construction Programme — 64

BUILD YOUR OWN
HOUSE

Contents

12. Construction Phase | 67

This chapter is divided into sections and in the correct sequence for managing your project

A. Enabling Works | 67

B. Site Setting Out | 69

C. Foundations | 70

D. Drainage | 79

E. Substructure And Floor Slabs | 89

F. Superstructure And Scaffold | 95

G. Roof | 106

H. First Fix | 115

I. Windows | 122

J. Plastering, Dry Lining and Rendering | 128

Contents

12. Construction Phase Continued — 132

K. Second Fix — 132

L. Decoration And Final Fix — 141

M. External Works — 145

N. Metering. Telephones and Media — 154

O. Sound And Air Test — 158

P. Checking And Ensuring Quality — 163

Q. Collating Certification & Commissioning — 176

R. Moving In — 196

13. Health and Safety — 200

14. Reclaiming VAT — 208

You And Your Project

Why self-build?

Here are just a few reasons: you like the idea of controlling your own project, you wish to monitor your expenditure as the project evolves or you may simply like to ensure that the work is carried out to a high standard and to your specifications. The most common theme is that people dream of one day building their own home. And why not? It can be hugely satisfying and rewarding. This book will give you the confidence and a suitable knowledge base to do just that.

Once you have an idea in your mind of what you would like to build, what's the next step to take?

There are many things to consider as a self-builder:-

Can I find the right plot in the right location?

How will I finance the project?

How much can I afford?

What design choices would satisfy the whole family's needs?

Let's take this one step at a time. Firstly, it might be a good idea to make a simple sketch of your project, or reference plans from existing buildings that you may wish to incorporate. Take into consideration how many bedrooms you require, parking and garaging; south-facing gardens are always more desirable too.

Location - this is all important. This is going to be your new home, a place where you want to live; if you choose the wrong location you are never going to be happy. Make sure you consider things like: is it easy to travel to work? Is it close to the local schools? Will I need to use public transport? Is it close to the amenities my family and I require?

Now you need to find a plot in the right location. Where is a good place to find plots for sale? A good starting place would be your local paper, looking in the property sections. Internet searches using sites such as '*right move*' and '*plot search*' are always good places to search for building plots, and local property auctions is another source.

You may wish to consider purchasing a dilapidated property and demolishing it. One small tip here - never demolish a structure until you have achieved planning permission, as going ahead without permission to demolish a property may lose any prospect of gaining planning rights, therefore, it is strongly advised to go through the correct channels here.

Can you afford it? This is probably the most important question of all. Lack of funding is possibly the most common problem with self-build projects. So I suggest before you begin, you need to prepare a feasible budget.

Having sufficient funds to complete your project is fundamental for success.

Your input. All self-builders will have their own idea of how much input they want in their own project. Everyone has their own skills and you need to recognise your own capabilities. This could be varied and you need to be honest with yourself.

When project-managing, the client will often say for example "we will do the decorating" and nine times out of ten this turns into a disaster and you end up finding qualified decorators to sort the project out. So decide what your input is going to be; something as simple as keeping your site clean and tidy throughout the duration of a project will save you a considerable amount of money.

> **Budget**
> Funding your self-build home is obviously an important factor to success. Be realistic and try to build in 15% reserve funds. Building projects seldom run exactly to budget .. and rarely below budget!

If you want to do no more than being the client, you need to get someone to manage your project. You three main options would be, using an Architectural Practice, appointing a Project Manager or engaging a builder.

If you decide to take on the role of Project Manager you will need to make sure you devote enough time to it, as it is a full time role, especially once you get into the construction phase.

This is what you can expect from the three main options:

Architectural Practice – They will be able to prepare plans and submit them for planning approval. Once successful at planning stage they will then be able to prepare construction drawings and add all the structural elements, making sure all drawings comply with current Building Regulations. Please note regulations are constantly changing; what was acceptable yesterday may not be acceptable today. Usually architects will only manage your project from a distance, in other words they will be office based and make few site visits. They would recommend and employ a builder on your behalf. If required, they would employ or recommend a Quantity Surveyor (QS).

Project Manager – This is a role some self-builders take on themselves. If this is a path you are considering you will need to have a good understanding of the construction industry, plus plenty of time. If you decide to hire a project manager this is what you can expect for your money. Firstly and very importantly he/she will be your direct contact with all the activities involved in your project. It is important that you keep him/her informed of any decisions you might make regarding your project, as one decision often effects other elements of a project. You can expect your project manager to liaise with planners, architects, building inspectors, sub contractors or builders all on your behalf.

Your Project Manager will also be heavily involved with your budget, although not all Project Managers prepare the budget; this often the job of a Quantity Surveyor. The project manager will also be involved in hiring of sub-contractors or a building contractor. He or she will then be responsible for monitoring their performance through the duration of the contract, making sure work is carried out to an agreed time frame and to an acceptable standard.

He/she will make sure all inspections are carried out as and when required. He/she will also organise the incoming services that are required: gas, water, electric and media, ensuring they are all laid in sequence with the construction programme, which he/she would have prepared. A construction programme is a useful tool as it is usually used to drive a project. A construction programme doesn't need to be complicated but it will give you an understanding of the duration of your project and what should be happening at any given time. This will become flexible and will be updated regularly. The project manager would also be responsible for collating all information required for obtaining an occupation certificate. More information about occupation certificates will be covered within the later stages of the construction phase section. You need to understand the importance of an occupation certificate as it can affect any borrowed money or the re-sale of a property.

What do project managers charge? They will either charge you an hourly rate or they will want a percentage of the total contract price, normally somewhere between 10% and 15%.

Engaging a builder – You may wish to go down this route; it has many advantages and disadvantages. The main advantage is that once you have agreed your scheme and agreed a quote, all the responsibilities of completing the project are left with the builder. The disadvantage of going down this route is that it would make your project far more contractual, giving you less control of your project. Be aware that any amendments you make to your scheme will be charged accordingly. These are normally referred to as EXTRAS. This is the area in which building contractors make most profit.

Example: Site location plan **1:1250 scale**

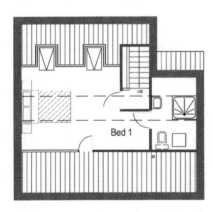

Proposed first floor plan

Proposed ground floor plan

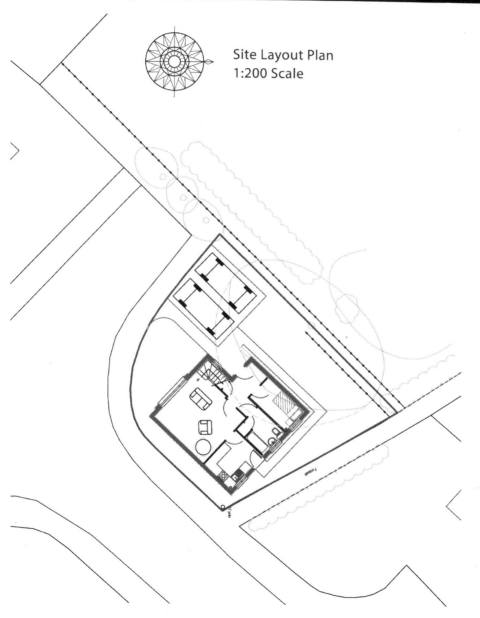

Site Layout Plan
1:200 Scale

2
Planning

Most self-builders will probably have purchased a site that already has the benefit of planning permission. Outline planning would require you to seek further approval of the design and layout including materials that you intend to use for full planning permission. If you have full planning permission you will not be required to seek any further approvals providing you choose to build to the approved set of drawings, but there could be conditions attached. It is usual for conditions to be attached and you will find that some are generic, i.e. a development must begin within 3 years of the approval date; otherwise a further application may be required.

Another condition may be, erection of fencing before a development can take place. Make sure you conform to all conditions and get them discharged accordingly. Failure to do this could result in being issued with an enforcement notice, which ultimately could result in you having your planning approval removed. However, most issues can normally be resolved without the planning department having to take any drastic action. Please note, planning approval is not enough for you to commence works on site; you do need to obtain building regulation-approval. (You will find more on this subject in the following sections).

Planning really is a mine field and unless you have any experience this task is best left to other people. Your two main choices would be an Architects Practice or a Planning Consultant.

Architects Practice – They will be able to do the whole package from design, preparing and submitting an application to satisfying any planning conditions. Most architects have dealt with the local planning departments and would normally have a good idea of their policy. Planning policy criteria does vary depending on which local authority you are dealing with.

Planning Consultants – Planning Consultants specialise more in planning law and are more useful when a planning application is more contentious. You will find that most planning consultants don't get involved in preparing plans, however they will use people to do this for them if required, and this may be an architect or a CAD designer.

DIY – You can submit an application yourself. This is best done by using the governments planning portal. There is plenty of information on the planning portal to guide you through the planning process and is obviously a cheaper option.

Planning consultation – Before submitting an application, your local authority will be happy to discuss your application with you. Planning consultants and architects will usually have a consultation with the planning department before submitting an application. At a consultation you will not get a planning decision but they will advise you on the merits of your application.

Submitting an application – To submit a planning application there is a criteria of information that is required. This does vary depending which local authority you are dealing with, but usually the following are required: a location plan - this has to be to scale as per local authority requirement. The site boundary needs to be outlined by way of marking it in red. North also needs to be indicated on the plan.

A Site Plan – This indicates the position of the proposed new dwelling in relation to roads, paths and surrounding buildings. You must also indicate North. A scale will also be required.

Design and access statement – This is a document that informs the planners of a number of things: the materials you intend using, site access, your sustainable approach to constructing your dwelling and environmental impact. You can also include other design information within the statement.

Floor Layouts – These will indicate how the proposed dwelling is to be divided up internally and clearly indicate the intentional use of each room, i.e. bedroom, kitchen etc.

Elevations – You will be required to show all four elevations and clearly mark them; it would be usual to name them according to what direction they are facing. Any other supporting documents are purely voluntary but useful in explaining the merits of your application.

Fee – This varies with the size of your application. If you are submitting your application online there is a fee calculator.

Once all these items have been submitted you will receive confirmation from your local authority that your application has been accepted. If any required elements of an application have not been submitted, your application will be rejected.

When your application has been accepted you will be allocated a case officer; all further correspondence will then be directed to your case officer. Make sure you always use the reference number that will be allocated to your case by the Local Planning Authority (LPA).

The best way to make a planning application is to do it online using the government planning portal. This can be found by going to:

www.planningportal.gov.uk

Anyone can register to use this service and there is a step-by-step guide you can follow to enable you to successfully submit your application. It will automatically, once complete, be submitted to the relevant planning authority.

Once your application has been validated the local authority will then invite Highways, parish council, and residents neighbouring your site to comment on your application. If all the replies received are favourable you could achieve planning from your planning officer by way of delegated powers. This means your application need not go in front of the planning committee.

If your application turns out to be contentious, then your application will have to go on a planning agenda and be decided by the planning committee. The case officer at this point will make his own recommendation to the committee. The planning officer's recommendation does carry a lot of weight and you will often find that planning decisions are made with the case officer's recommendation. The planning committee is made up from locals who are not professional in the field of planning.

Planning committee agendas are posted on the local authorities' website and it is usually up to the planning committee as to the date of the meeting when your application is to be determined. At the planning committee meeting, you can attend and also have an opportunity to explain to the committee why you think your application should be approved. There could also be people there who will voice their opinion as to why they think your application should be rejected. The committee will usually approve or reject your application at this meeting, but it has been known for the committee to request further information regarding your application.

If your application is approved, you will be issued with an approval notice together with your submitted plans stamped with an approval; these approved plans must be kept safe, as they would be the plans required by solicitors or finance companies as proof of planning approval. It would not be advisable to use the drawings that are officially stamped as approved whilst working on site. Make duplicate copies to distribute while constructing your home. (You will find you will have to distribute many copies of your plans to all the various trades for their use).

Amendments to Approved Plans
Once you have achieved planning consent and before you commence your project, or maybe during the construction phase, you may wish to make amendments to your plans. You must inform the planning department; this is initially best achieved by having a meeting with the planning case officer, who has been allocated to your application. The planning officer at this point will advise you if your amendments will require a further application. Minor amendments can usually be approved, if acceptable, by the case officer. However you will be required to submit a new set of plans showing any amendments, and there will be a fee. If the case officer considers your amendments are potentially controversial, especially with neighbours he may require a new application. At this point if you are to resubmit a new application it would be advisable to stop any activities on the construction of your home.

The three main applications required by the planning department regarding amendments are as follows –

Non Material Change – An example of this would be if you wanted to change a door position.

Material Change – An example would be if you wanted to use a different type of brick or roof tile.

New Applications – This would be required if there were any major alterations to your project. These may include a change of roof design or enlarging the building.

It is worth noting that conservatories do not require planning permission, unless they are over a certain size.

Appeals – If your application gets rejected, the planning department will list the reasons. If you can rectify and remove the reasons from your application by way of replanning your development, you can re-submit your application free of charge. (Each application is only allowed one free re-submission).

If your application gets rejected again, you can then start an Appeal process. This is a long and drawn out process and on average it takes about 26 weeks to obtain a decision. You can find plenty of guidance regarding planning appeals on the government planning portal website.

Appeals
It's a fact that only 1 in 3 appeals are successful

There are two main types of appeal . ..

Written representation – This is where all correspondence is made in writing to an appeal officer, who will be allocated to your case. You appeal directly in writing to the appeal officer stating the reasons you feel your application should be approved and, in turn, the planning department that have refused your application will make their recommendations why they feel your application should be rejected.

Hearing – This would be heard at a local venue, normally at the local planning authority's offices, village halls or community centres. Hearings are open to members of the public and an inspector will invite all parties to express their opinions.

If you are still refused planning at an appeal you will have to change your scheme if you still want to pursue planning approval.

Example: Elevations **1:1250 scale**

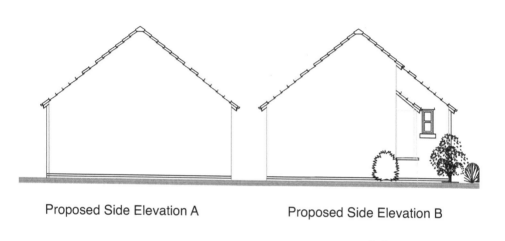

Proposed Side Elevation A   Proposed Side Elevation B

Proposed Rear Elevation   Proposed Front Elevation

The cost of any development is probably the most important factor, as it is not the norm for anyone to have unlimited funds. Working out the cost of building your project is crucial to most self-builders.

You will find that you have three areas of expenditure

1 – The cost of purchasing your site

2 – The cost of achieving planning permission.

3 – The construction costs.

Purchasing your site: Self-builders will usually purchase a site that already has the benefit of planning, as there are real risks associated with purchasing land and then trying to achieve planning. Even if your site does have planning there are still many other factors to consider that could be a very costly addition to the total cost of your development. Here are a few things to look out for when buying land that already has the benefit of planning approval :–

Can you easily connect to main drainage? If not you will need to consider installing a sewage treatment plant, or extensive laying of drainage to link up with the nearest main drainage system, which in turn could involve installing a pumping station. (You will find more information of these options in the drainage section). What are the ground conditions? Is the site contaminated and in need of remediation? This can prove very costly.

How far away are the nearest services? Gas, Water, Electric and media? It can be very costly getting services connected to a new property especially over distance. You will find that utility companies have no obligation to supply a new service to your property without incurring infrastructure costs payable by you.

Infrastructure: Usually refers to roads, services and main drainage. Are there any Way leaves or covenants attached to the land? Your solicitor, however, should make you aware of these.

Way Leaves are rights people have to cross your land. Where this relates to a utility company they might have rights to excavate. Way leaves should be registered with land registry.

Covenants: Usually an agreement, contract or written promise made between an owner and a successive owner which usually restricts certain activities happening on the land in question. This could be a restriction on building. It is worth noting that covenants can be hard to enforce, particularly with the passage of time. If you wish to build on a piece of land that has a covenant against it you can normally take out an indemnity policy with an insurance company.

These items would all be considered to be additional to your construction costs - in other words a builder would not normally include such costs when estimating a price for constructing a dwelling.

The cost of achieving Planning Permission: This can become very costly. Here are some of the costs involved in achieving planning:

1 – The cost of having your drawings prepared, including site and location plans, floor layouts and elevations. Please note you will also need further drawings for your building regulation approval which is separate from planning.

2 – Planning fees: This is the cost of actually submitting an application; this fee varies depending on the size of the site. Currently a fee for full planning consent is £335 depending on the gross floor area of the dwelling. More information on planning fees can be found on the governments planning portal website.

3 – Planning consultants: These are usually engaged when a planning application would be seen to be contentious. They do not normally provide drawings but will be able to have these prepared on your behalf. They normally specialise in planning law and will be able to advise you on such planning matters.

 A good planning consultant will also be able to advise you on the prospects of your planning application being approved. You will find planning consultants are a costly expense but they can also prove to be invaluable.

4 - Design technicians: This group are getting ever more popular especially with major house builders, most will use computer aided design (CAD). Not all design technicians will submit planning applications.

Construction Costs - This will be your project's most variable cost as there are so many different factors to be considered. There are also many ways of working out build costs; the most popular one you will hear is a price *per square metre* or *square foot* of floor space. This formula is used by house builders, and particularly house builders that use the same model houses and build in large multiples. If you look at the houses they build you will notice that regardless of the size they will all be built using similar construction methods and of similar if not the same materials. This way they can work out the size of house they can build at a square metre/foot rate. It's noticeable in meetings with house builders that they analyse this cost and try to work out ways of reducing the build costs. This is a whole different ball game than just building a one off house, unless of course you are to compare costs of another house that has been built to the same specification.

Another thing that house builders don't include in their build costs is infrastructure costs, roads, sewers etc. Their infrastructure costs are usually included in site purchase costings. Recently, while speaking to a QS friend of mine who works for a major builder, he informed me that his company were currently building for £72 per square foot. This rate would bear no relationship to anything you may build, so my advice would be not to use price per square foot/metre as a guide.

There are major things to consider when costing your project, Here are the main areas to concentrate on:

1 - Enabling works: This is the cost of preparing your site ready for construction. Are trees to be removed? Does the ground require remediation? Is there good access to the site? There are many reasons why ground has to be remediated. If previously used for parking it might be contaminated with hydrocarbons. If your site has Japanese knotweed, remediation for the removal of knotweed is not only expensive it is also time-consuming.

Another reason for remediation works would be if your site had previously been used for landfill. All forms of remediation usually require a specialist contractor to carry out the work. How accessible is your site? If it is not accessible for deliveries you will almost certainly incur extra costs in getting materials on site.

2 – Foundations: You will need to have a soil survey carried out to determine which type of foundation is suitable for your site. This will be dependent on substructure and ground conditions. There is no such thing as a standard foundation, so the cost will vary significantly. Foundations will be covered in depth in a later chapter.

3- Oversight slab: The design is dependant upon your foundation design, as in some designs, mainly a raft, the oversight slab will be incorporated in the foundation design.

4- Superstructure: There are many different variations in costs depending on the design of your superstructure. A more traditional approach i.e. block work and face brick, or block and render, works out cheaper than timber frame. External wall finishes like natural stone cladding can be very costly.

5 - Roofs and roof coverings: Roof trusses are generally cheaper to buy and install then traditionally-constructed roofs. By traditionally-constructed roofs I mean roofs constructed out of loose timbers. By introducing dormers, lower rooves and pediments increase roof construction costs. Roof coverings can vary from expensive Westmorland natural slate to cheap concrete tiles.

6 - Doors and windows: The cost can vary from standard UPVC windows and doors to non-standard hardwood windows and doors.

7 - Internals: There are many cost factors to consider here. Do you want hardwood staircase, skirtings and architraves or are you happy to use cheaper softwood or MDF? There is also a huge difference between internal doors and door furniture. A price of a door can easily vary from £15 to £200. Plumbing, depending on your plumbing system and quality of sanitary ware, will significantly alter costs. Electrics is not just the amount of sockets you should take into

BUILD YOUR OWN
HOUSE

consideration but also the required finish of the switch and socket plates; the type of lighting, do you want wall lights or fancy down lighters? These are all things that need to be considered. Decoration: are you just aiming for a builders finish? By this I mean white ceilings and woodwork with walls in magnolia, or are you going for wallpaper, coving varnished or stained woodwork? There are also huge differences in the costs of kitchens and sanitary ware.

8 - External works: Are you having garden walls built or landscaped gardens? Perhaps you are going for turf or even just seeding.

As you can see, from this brief account the cost implications to any project can vary enormously, so it is important to have some idea of what your construction budget is going to be.

Working out the costs

There are two essential elements to working out build costs.

1 – Specification (in the profession you will hear it being referred to as a spec)

2 – Bill of Quantities

Specification : Your specification needs to include all the components that make up your dwelling, you will find some of this information on your building regulation - for example, drawings, type of foundation, superstructure details, roof details. Then you will have to decide on things like kitchens, sanitary ware, the type of skirting and architrave you are going to use, doors and windows including handles and locks (usually referred to as door and window furniture), type of heating system, electrics, including type of lighting and finishes to sockets and switches and decorating.

Just look around your house inside and out and make a list of all the components you wish to incorporate into your new house. The more information you can put into specification the more accurate your projected costs will be.

Bill of quantities: A bill of quantities is usually prepared by a Quantity Surveyor (QS). A QS will need a full specification and a set of building regulation drawings to enable him/her to prepare a bill of quantities. A bill of quantities will combine materials, labour and any other associated construction costs, like plant and material taken off site, to enable him/her to come up with a total build cost.

Can you prepare the bill of quantities yourself? The answer is yes but it's not recommended , as you really do need detailed construction knowledge. It is far more involved than just measuring, it would also include items like mobilisation of plant and bulking up material that has to be taken off site. Some of the larger builders merchants do offer a service for quantifying the materials. This then enables you to add in the labour costs and any other associated costs that need to be added in to give you a total cost for your project. When preparing a bill of quantities if there are any unknowns, for example you may not have chosen your kitchen, you will see that whoever is preparing your bill will just put a Prime Cost, known as a PC unit against the item, this would be an amount allocated to the item. Another cost that must be considered is the cost of managing your project. Even if you decide to manage your project yourself there will be a huge time element, and as the old saying goes "Time is Money".

	Steel Lintel 100mm box...	Large raising pieces	0.00
Drains	Universal Raising Piece 700mm	Basement shuttering	54.84
Foundations	BBA OSB3 2400 x 1200 x 15mm	Basement	27.42
	Kingspan K3 Insulation Board 2400 x 1200 x 70mm	Basement walls	23.69
	R'mix Concrete GEN 1, 125mm slump 2-3 m3 (Allowance £85)	Basement conc	13.71
	Steel Reinforcement Mesh 4.8 x 2.4m B785		
Oversite and slabbing	Sharp Sand Bulk Bag	Sand for grouting between blocks	0.62
Drains	PC Soakaway Unit with Double Step Irons 1050mm Diameter x 1000mm	Deep soakaway sections	2.00
Oversite and slabbing	Blue Circle Mastercrete Original Cement 25kg Bag	Cement for grouting between blocks	12.34
	Building Sand Bulk Bag	Sand blinding to slab	8.90
	Concrete Floor Beam 150mm	Concrete floor beams	111.60
	Flooring Grade Polystyrene Insulation Sheet 2400 x 1200 x 25mm	Perimeter insulation	0.00
	Kingspan K3 Insulation Board 2400 x 1200 x 70mm	Insulation to underside of slab	54.63
	Periscope Wall/Floor Vent	Cranked ventilators	0.00
	Pitch Polymer DPC 100mm x 20m	Beam and block DPC	0.0
	Polythene DPM Black 300mu 4 x 25m BBA (27.6kg)	DPM or radon membrane	0.0
	Polythene DPM Blue 300mu 4 x 25m PIFA (27.6kg)	DPM to concrete slab	0.0
	R'mix Concrete GEN 1, 125mm slump 2-3 m3 (Allowance £85)	Concrete infill	0
	R'mix Concrete RC 30, 50mm slump 6m3 (Allowance £75)		0

4
Finance

Having the money to finance your project and knowing how much money you need is a key consideration for any project. Before you even start looking at options for sourcing finance you should first see if the project is viable. This is the very first step any developer would take. If the project doesn't turn out to be viable, it would be advisable not to proceed any further at that point.

VIABILITY ASSESSMENT

DATE:

SCHEME NUMBER:

DETAILS

Site Address:	
Owner:	
Architect:	
Agent:	
Proposal:	

SITE PREPARATION — COST

	COST
Purchase:	£
Solicitor:	£
Interest:	£
Demolition &/or Site Clearance:	£
Reinstatement:	£
Roads & Sewers:	£
Services:	£
Abnormals :	£
	£

DEVELOPMENT — COST

	COST
Build:	£
Agents Fees:	£
Architect Fees:	£
Solicitors Fees:	£
Abnormals:	£
Interest:	£

TOTALS — COST

	COST
Sales:	£
Cost:	£
Profit:	£

A typical Viability Assessment Document

As you can see there is a sales cost included. By sales cost I mean a market valuation of a completed dwelling. This would be required if you were applying for a self-build mortgage.

So let's take the scenario, you have found a plot to purchase with the benefit of planning permission. You have done a viability study and the costs seem to stack up.

So where do you get finance from?

1 – You have sold an existing property and you have the funds to finance your project

2 – You have decided to borrow money against an existing property

3 – You have your own funds available to finance your project

4 – You have friends or family to finance your project

If you have none of the above you will probably require a mortgage

There are mortgage companies that specialise in self-build mortgages; however you will need to meet the same criteria as you would if obtaining a normal mortgage, as you will be required to prove your ability to pay back any borrowed money.

Self-build mortgages work in a different way; firstly they will normally require at least a 25% deposit of the combined cost of land plus construction.

Example £100,000 to purchase land + £100,000 to construct property = £200,000. A minimum deposit of £50,000 would be required. You will find lenders vary on the size of deposit that is required.

Note you will find the bigger the deposit you have the more attractive the mortgage deal will be.

We have compiled a list of lenders on the next page .. . Please note that this list should only be used as guide as these figures are changeable.

4
Finance

Lender's details		Loan to value on land	Stage required for first payment	Loan to value during construction	Final loan to value land and building
BM Solutions	bmsolutions.co.uk	Max 75%	Land	Max 75%	Max 75%
Chorley & District BS	0845 223 4888	Max 85%	Land	Max 85%	Max 80%
Cumberland BS	0800 032 3030	Max 75%	Negotiable	Max 75%	Max 85%
Darlington	01325 366366	Max 70%	Land	Max 70%	Max 70%
Dudley BS	01384 231414	Max 50%	Damp course	Max 75%	Max 75%
Earl Shinton BS	01455 844422	Max 50%	Land	Max 75%	Nax 75%
Ecology BS	0845 674 5566	Max 85%	Land	Max 85%	Max 85%
Furness BS	0800 834312	Max 66%	Land	Max 66%	Max 80%
Halifax	0845 727 3747	Not on land	First floor level	Max 80%	Max 80%
Hanley Economic BS	0845 223 4888	75%	Land	Max 75%	Max 75%
Hinckley & Rugby BS	0800 870 9499	Not on land	Footings	Max 75%	Max 75%
Holmesdale BS	01737 245716	Not on land	Damp proof	Max 60%	Max 70%
Ipswich BS	0845 230 8686	Max 75%	Negotiable	Max 75%	Max 75%
Leeds BS	01845 050 5062	Max 75%	Land	Max 75%	Max 80%
Lloyds TSB Scotland	0800 0560156	Max 50%	Land	Max 75%	Max 75%
Loughborough BS	01509 631950	Max 75%	Sill level	Max 75%	Max 75%
Mansfield	01623 676345	Max 75%	Wall plate level	Max 75%	Max 75%
Melton Mowbray	01664 414141	Not on land	Footings	Max 75%	Max 75%
Newbury BS	01635 555777	Max 66%	Land	Max 75%	Max 75%
Northern Rock BS	0800 0285 277	Not on land	Roofed & tiled	Max 85%	Max 85%
Norwich & Peterborough BS	0845 300 2522	Max 80%	Land	Max 80%	Max 80%
Nottingham BS	0115 956 4716	Not on land	Eaves	Max 65%	Max 90%
Progressive BS	028 9024 4926	Max 60%	Land	Max 70%	Max 75%
Saffron BS	0800 072 1100	Max 75%	Land	Max 75%	Max 75%
Scottish BS	0131 3137700	Max 80%	Land	Max 80%	Max 80%
Tipton & Coseley	0800 833853	Max 60%	Land	Max 60%	Max 60%
Ulster Bank	ulsterbank.com	Not on land	First floor level	Max 90%	Max 90%
Vernon BS	0161 429 6262	Max 75%	Land	Max 75%	Max 75%
West Brom BS	0845 456 7418	Max 50%	Footings	Max 75%	Max 75%

Charges
Mortgage companies charge for every site visit to assess each stage of valuation!

How a self-build mortgage works.

Your lender will advance you money at each stage of your project. This will usually be done by the lender sending out a surveyor to do a valuation of your project and advance you money based on the valuation. This would be the same process until your project is complete. They will normally only advance you any money relating to the current value of your build.

Your first advance would normally be made if requested once your foundations have been completed. After that you can usually ask for valuations at any further stages. But beware, mortgage companies do charge for each visit a surveyor makes to undertake a valuation.

On completion of your project you will be given a period of time in which you have to convert your self-build mortgage to a repayment mortgage. You can often have this put in place, prior to the completion of your project.

Make sure you budget properly when raising money to self-build, as lenders will not exceed the amount of money they lend against a current valuation of your project.

Below are some of the main requirements that lenders will need you to have in place prior to them releasing any funds:

Copies of full planning approval

Land registry documents

Approved building regulation drawings

Structural warranty in place

Once planning approval has been achieved and before you commence any construction activities on site, you will need to have building regulation approval in place. Building regulation approval is totally separate from planning approval.

Building regulation approval is a requirement to ensure you are going to construct your property in a manner that conforms to current building regulations. A separate set of drawings are usually required that will show all current approved methods of construction relating to your project.

Who produces building regulation drawings?

This is done by either your architect or your designer; they in turn might have to outsource some of the required information, i.e. foundation design and any structural elements that may be required, for example structural steelwork and roof construction.

Once your architect/designer has collated all this information he or she will be able to produce a set of working drawings that can be submitted for approval.

Submitting Building Regulation Drawings for approval.

This is unlike obtaining planning approval; it is not deemed to be contentious and doesn't have to be heard by a committee.

It is simply an application that has to be submitted with a fee. It will require a full set of working drawings, which then goes through the process of being checked. If the inspector is happy with the drawings he will approve them. Sometimes they might require further information before they will approve certain aspects of the design, but you will usually find that the inspectors are happy to work with you and give you advice if required.

At one time Building Regulation Approval had to be submitted to Local Authority Building Control (LABC). Now you can use any firm of approved inspectors that might be available in your area. These are totally independent from the local authority, but Local Authority Building control is still by far the most popular avenue. If you *do* use an independent approved inspector and not LABC approved

L.A.B.C.

You must inform the Local Authority Building Control before your project starts, even if you intend using an independent inspector.

you must still inform LABC in advance of starting your project. If you fail to do this you will lose your rights to use an independent inspector.

Fees vary depending on which route you decide to take, but the process is still the same. The fees are broken down into two parts.

1
A fee will be charged for having the plans checked, to ensure that they conform to current building regulations

2
A fee will be charged for an inspector to come out to site at key construction phases to inspect and ensure you are complying with your approved drawings and carrying out all work to approved construction methods and standards

The key stage inspections are usually as follows: pre-start, excavation of foundations, damp proof course, drainage, superstructure and completion. Additional inspections may be required depending on your project. An additional inspection would be necessary if you are introducing any retaining structures to your development.

After each inspection the inspector will inform you if it is OK to carry on with your project. If he or she is unhappy with an inspection they will inform you what is required to satisfy the inspection and will probably want to revisit. Never carry on with your project if you have not had a key stage satisfactory inspection, as you will find you may have difficulty getting your project signed off at the end.

Some of the key information that is required when submitting your drawings for planning approval:

Drainage
You must clearly indicate your method of discharging both surface water and foul water away from your property.

BUILD YOUR OWN
HOUSE

Foul Water

Foul water can be discharged by connecting straight into an existing main sewer, or by introducing a waste treatment plant, but please note that waste treatment plants still require an outfall to take away water, the water will be deemed to be clean after passing through the plant.

Another option to remove foul water from your property could be by constructing a pumping station. This would only be necessary if you had to pump sewerage uphill as most systems rely on gravity.

Pumping stations are very costly to construct and have a complicated adoption process. When constructing a single dwelling it should be discounted if at all possible.

Surface Water

Surface water (rain water) can usually be discharged away from your property in one of two ways. If possible your best and cheapest option is to gain approval to discharge into an existing drainage system. If this is not possible then it may be necessary to construct a soak away, which usually involves digging a hole at least five metres from your property, filling it with hard core or a suitable aggregate and capping it with a material that won't allow any small aggregate to contaminate the hard core - this would usually be a PVC type of product. Finally, landscaping over the top to complete.

If you are going down the route of constructing soakaways then a permeability test would have to be carried out to show the required capacity of your soakaway. I will talk more about carrying out permeability tests in the drainage section.

Foundations

A foundation design will be required. Foundations must be designed to take into account the ground conditions that you are intending to build over. To determine a foundation design, you would normally dig some test holes to enable you to have your foundations designed. There are many different foundation designs and these will vary depending on the ground conditions. I will go into more detail on the subject in the foundation section, but foundations are fundamentally one of the most import parts of any project to get right; it is very costly and difficult to rectify badly designed foundations.

DPC (Damp Proof course)
All Damp Proof courses and membranes must be indicated on your drawings.

Floor Slab
The construction details of a floor slab would be required. This might require some additional structural details and details of any reinforcing that may have to be introduced.

Wall Construction
The method of wall construction must be indicated on your drawings, clearly showing or stating any insulation that is to be used.

Joists and Roofs
Floor joist layouts backed up with structural calculations will be required. This also applies to the roof construction. You will find that if you go down the route of using a roof truss manufacturer they will also provide you with a set of structural calculations.

This is just a brief description of information that would be shown on a set of building regulation drawings, but it is worth noting that different projects will require information which is specific to that project.

Additional Information that is required as part of building regulation approval:

SAP Rating
All dwellings need to be rated and constructed in a way that allows them to perform efficiently. You need to know how much energy will be used and how much carbon dioxide will be emitted. This is known as a SAP rating, which stands for Standard Assessment Procedure. There is a required level that has to be adhered to; your architect or designer will be well aware of what rating he/she

needs to achieve and will design your property accordingly. Building control will require a set of calculations along with a EPC (Energy Performance Certificate). SAP is a government compliance tool.

Gas Safe Certificate
A Gas Safe Certificate is required if gas is to be installed in your dwelling. It is issued after all the gas appliances i.e. gas hobs, boilers and gas fires have been installed and commissioned by your gas engineer. He will then issue you with a gas safe certificate of which a copy has to be passed on to building control. It is essential that if you are to have gas installed into your property you make sure you employ a plumber that is registered to enable him to issue you with a Gas Safe Certificate.

Electrical Test Certificate
An Electrical Test Certificate will be required upon completion of all electrical installations, a copy of which will have to passed on to Building Control. Once again, ensure your electrician issues a test certificate on completion of your project.

Sometimes you will have more than one contractor carrying out electrical installations to your property. An example of this may be if you have one contractor installing all the lighting and sockets to your property and another contractor wiring up all the heating controls. In this instance you would require two separate test certificates, as each contractor would only be liable for carrying out the installation of his own work, as contracted.

Contaminated Land
You will be required to prove that your site is in a condition that it is perfectly safe to inhabit. This would require soil analysis. Nowadays a lot of land we build on has been previously used as something different from residential, for example it could have been a garage or perhaps a factory unit. In these instances some of the ground may have become contaminated with oil (more usually referred to as hydrocarbons) or possibly asbestos. In these instances your site would have to be remediated to satisfy Building Control that it is fit to inhabit.

If you find that remediation has to be carried out to your site, you will then have to provide a validation certificate. Validation certificates are provided by specialist contractors.

Japanese Knotweed is another problem. Nowadays it is widespread across the country and can cause havoc to a dwelling. If your plot does contain Japanese Knotweed, ensure it is removed correctly and by a specialist contractor. You will find that the process of validating a site that is contaminated with Knotweed is a lengthy process which can run into many months.

In all cases when dealing with contaminated land be aware that it can be very costly and cause long delays to actually being able to build your dwelling.

Japanese Knotweed

Japanese knotweed develops an extensive network of underground shoots called rhizomes. Rhizomes tend to grow laterally, spreading out from the crown of the plant.

Research indicates that lateral extension from the parent plant can reach 7 metres and that it can grow to a depth of 3 metres.

However, this can vary considerably and will depend on the nature and history of the site.

Note: Consider the cost of any remediation work that may be required to your plot before purchase.

Approved Documents

Building regulations are based on a set of guidance documents known as Approved Documents. These documents are in 14 separate parts:

Part A – Structural stability
Part B – Fire precautions
Part C – The prevention of dampness
Part D – Toxic substances
Part E – Sound resistance of walls and floors between dwellings
Part F – Ventilation of habitable rooms and unheated voids
Part G – Hygiene
Part H – Drainage and waste disposal
Part J – Heating appliances
Part K – Stairways
Part L – Conservation of fuel and power
Part M – Access to building and facilities for disabled people
Part N – The safe positioning of glazing in windows
Part P – Electrical safety

All these documents can be viewed on the government's planning portal website. These documents are constantly reviewed and updated, so make sure you are referring to the latest documented revisions.

The guidance documents contain practical ways and explanations of how to comply with the functional requirements of the building regulations.

It is important to remember that Building Control not only approves drawings, they also monitor the methods and practices on site. Always try and strike up a good working relationship with your inspector as you will find they normally have an invaluable amount of knowledge, which they will usually be happy to share and will advise on any issues which you may encounter, relating to your project.

Code For Sustainable Homes

The Code For Sustainable Homes will be taken into consideration by your architect or your designer while he/she is producing your building regulation drawings.

The Code For Sustainable Homes is the national standard for the sustainable design and construction of new homes. The aim of the code is to reduce carbon emissions and promote a higher standard of sustainable design above the current minimum standards set out by the building regulations.

The code was launched by the Department for Communities and Local Government on 13 December 2006.

The code measures the whole home as a complete package assessing its sustainability against nine categories:

Energy/carbon dioxide

Water

Materials

Surface water run-off (flood prevention)

Waste

Pollution

Health and well-being

Management

Ecology

It uses a 1- 6 star system to rate the overall sustainability performance of a new home against these nine categories, 1 star is the least efficient with 6 stars being the most efficient.

The rating your home receives depends on how it measures up in these nine categories.

Once all this information has been collated an EPC (Energy Performance Certificate) can be produced. This is a requirement to enable you to get your house signed off after completion.

You can obtain a free technical guide that sets out the requirements of the latest version of the code and how code assessment is reached from:

www.gov.uk/government/publications
/code-for-sustainable-homes-technical-guidance

There are many ways you can ensure that your new home performs efficiently. Here are some of the more common methods used in ensuring new dwellings perform more efficiently:

Insulation - Insulating your new property correctly is by far the cheapest and most effective way of ensuring your home is performing effectively. If you compare the cost of the insulation against your fuel savings you will find insulation has the quickest payback period. The more insulation you introduce into your new property the better it will perform. Your architect or designer will have all insulation types and thicknesses indicated on your building regulation drawings. Insulation will be incorporated in the construction of the floor slab, all external walls, roof spaces and roof voids.

Glazing - Double glazing is now recognised as a minimum standard and it is not an uncommon practice to see triple glazing installed.

Heating systems and heating controls - There are now many types of heating systems on the market. You must carefully consider which system best suits your requirements, mainly dependent on the type of fuel that you are likely to be using. Gas is probably still the cheapest fuel and gas boilers are the most common forms of generating heat into properties, but there are other heating systems you may wish to consider.

Ground source heat pump - This is far cheaper to run than a conventional gas boiler however it is very expensive to install. It works by extracting heat from the ground; by the use of a heat exchanger the system will heat your home and your domestic water. This system requires electricity to run the heat exchanger but is not as costly as running a conventional boiler system, therefore it is considered more sustainable.

Underfloor heating - This is considered to be more efficient than traditional radiators, but once again it comes at an additional cost.

Biomass boilers - An environmentally-friendly form of heating due to the lack of Co2 emissions. They are popular if you are building in an area which doesn't benefit from mains gas. Biomass is cheaper and more environmentally-friendly than oil, propane or electric heating, although the cost of the boiler is much higher and requires constant monitoring.

Heating controls - An important consideration in the design of a heating system; the more thermostatic controls introduced to a system the more efficiently a system will perform. In an ideal situation you will be able to control the temperature of each room individually, which will save you the expense of unnecessarily having to heat areas that are not inhabited.

Photovoltaic panels - or PV as they are more commonly known are getting very popular. PV panels are usually mounted on the roof. PV panels convert sunlight into electricity. Any excess electricity that is produced can sold back to the national grid; this is achieved by having an inverter fitted, which can only be done by a registered MCS installer. You will find that the payback period for having PV installed is estimated to be at least 15 years.

Wind turbines - Wind turbines are used to produce additional electricity. The amount of electricity produced depends on many different factors: the size of the turbine, where the turbine is sited, and local wind conditions.

Like PV, if you want to sell unused electricity back to National Grid the system will have to be installed by a MCS accredited installer. The payback time in terms of how much electricity can be produced can, in some instances, be as short as six years.

Under permitted development rights in some cases it is possible to install domestic wind turbines without the need for a planning application, so long as specified limits and conditions are met. You will find more information specifying limits and conditions on the government's planning portal website. If you are intending to install a wind turbine to your house, building regulations will normally apply. The size, weight and the force exerted on all fixed points would be considered.

Solar thermal - Solar thermal panels are usually mounted on the roof and are similar in size to PV panels. Solar thermal panels are designed solely to heat your hot water and the panels are directly linked to your hot water cylinder. In many ways they are more efficient than PV as your hot water can be stored. They are much cheaper to install than PV and the payback period may be only a few years. There are also grants available for part of the installation cost for solar thermal panels.

Solar Thermal - Domestic Hot Water System

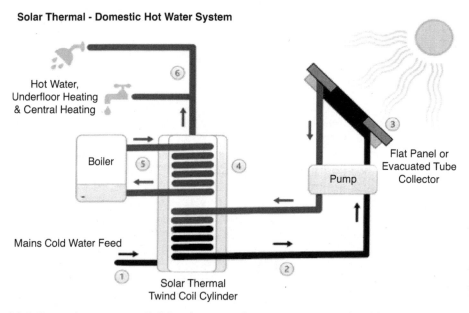

Hot Water, Underfloor Heating & Central Heating

Boiler

Mains Cold Water Feed

Pump

Flat Panel or Evacuated Tube Collector

Solar Thermal Twind Coil Cylinder

Lighting – Low energy lighting has now become very popular. Your electrician or an electrical wholesaler will be able to advise you when purchasing lighting to suit your project. Current building regulations state that a minimum of 75% of lighting in a new build has to be low energy.

Rain Water Harvesting – The idea of a rainwater harvester is to collect the rainwater and re-use it domestically. The water that falls on the roof is directed into a holding tank. When water is required the stored water is pumped through a UV filter making it ready for use. It is not recommended that this water is used for drinking or cooking, however some systems claim the water is pure enough to drink.

Harvested water is mainly used to flush toilets, run washing machines, and can be used to service an outside tap.

You will still require a mains water supply laid to your property, mainly for the use of drinking water and cooking purposes, plus water for personal hygiene. Most rainwater harvesting systems have a control panel which will automatically switch your water supply from the harvester to a mains supply if your tank becomes empty due to lack of rainfall.

Rain Water Harvesting System
You will receive a reduction on your water bill if you have a harvester installed, however the payback period could well run to many years, as the expenditure on purchase and installation of a harvester will add considerably to your costs.

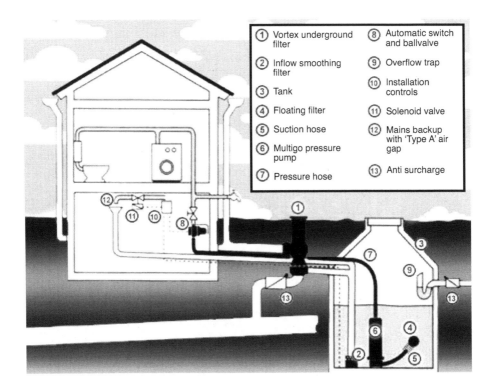

1. Vortex underground filter
2. Inflow smoothing filter
3. Tank
4. Floating filter
5. Suction hose
6. Multigo pressure pump
7. Pressure hose
8. Automatic switch and ballvalve
9. Overflow trap
10. Installation controls
11. Solenoid valve
12. Mains backup with 'Type A' air gap
13. Anti surcharge

BUILD YOUR OWN
HOUSE

Air Tightness - Air leakage is now taken into consideration while calculating the overall performance of a new build property. While your property is being constructed you must ensure the correct installation of doors, windows, meter boxes and plumbing pipes that are installed through the external walls; if all these are installed correctly it will prevent air leakage from your property.

Once your property has been completed it will require an air test to insure it complies. All new properties now have to comply and the results of the air test are taken into consideration when producing an EPC (Energy Performance Certificate).

Your architect or designer will take into consideration, while designing your property, what is known as Passive Solar Design. This maximises free heat gained from the sun.

For compliance with the code for sustainable homes more guidance can be found in the building regulations section, which deals with conservation of fuel and power.

You might have heard about the government-backed **Green Deal Scheme**, which is a loan that is repaid by way of increases to your electricity bill and is designed to enable the home owner to pay for improving the energy performance of their home. This loan is not available for new build properties.

A Warranty generally is a guarantee or promise which provides assurance by one party to another. When constructing a new dwelling you will need to have a Structural Guarantee in place. If you are in the process of trying to obtain funding this will almost certainly be required. Likewise if you are going to sell your dwelling, once it has been built a new purchaser would almost certainly require a Structural Guarantee in place.

Warranty IMPORTANT. This is something you need to have in place before you start your project.

If you have already built your dwelling without a structural warranty in place and you find you are required to provide one you will then need what is known as a Retrospective Warranty. There are very few insurance providers that are happy to provide you with one of these. If you can find a provider the premiums are usually very high due to the risk of providing insurance on a dwelling that has not been inspected during key stages of construction.

Listed are companies that will sell you Structural Warranties:

Self-Build Zone
LABC (Local Authority Building Control)
BLP (Building Life Plan)
Premier Guarantee
NHBC (National House Building Council)

Alternatively you can use an Architect's Certificate, which involves having your architect guarantee your project. This is not an insurance policy, but involves getting your Architect to issue a signed statement (upon completion) that he has inspected your dwelling whilst being built and is happy that the structural elements of your dwelling conform to accepted building practices. After completion if there were to be any structural problems with your property and you were going down the route of an Architects Certificate, you would then have to claim against the Architects' Professional Indemnity Insurance.

Warranties

Most lenders will require you to have a Structural Warranty in place before they will release any funds against your project.

NHBC and LABC both require that you become registered with them and that you are competent to use their insurance services. Fees for the registration would normally apply, along with proof of competence.

Warranty providers all have their own designated inspectors, who work totally independently from building control, so you will find that when you require building control to undertake an inspection you will also have to inform your warranty provider who will send out one of their own inspectors.

What your Structural Guarantee covers:

You will need to read your policy as the cover may vary, but mainly a structural warranty will cover:

FOUNDATIONS - DRAINAGE - SUPERSTRUCTURE - FLOOR JOISTS - ROOFS - WATERPROOFING

(waterproofing, meaning that all damp membranes are built in correctly)

You will find that some insurance companies will offer you additional cover, such as:

Cost of demolition to allow for the property to be rebuilt
Design and other fees in connection with any re-instatement
Costs of removing, storing and re-installing the contents of a property
Costs of providing alternative accommodation during the period of re-instatement

Most structural warranties last for the first 10 years upon completion of a new dwelling, although you can obtain extensions on these to 15 years, but they are rarely asked for. Architect's Certificates are only valid for the first 6 years.

Your nominated insurance provider will not issue you with a structural warranty until you obtain a completion certificate from whoever you are using for building control. Your nominated insurance provider will then issue you with your warranty

- this certificate will then be required by your mortgage lender.

This certificate is often referred to as a CML (Council of Mortgage Lenders).Always check that whoever you are using to provide your structural warranty is approved by your mortgage lender.

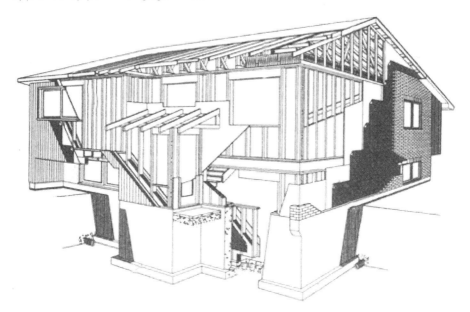

UK structural warranty companies:

Budget

The preparation and monitoring of a budget for your project is one of the keys for self-build success. Get your budget wrong and the consequences can be very punishing. A mis-managed budget is one of the most common reasons for self-builds not being completed successfully.

There are many aspects of your project to be considered when preparing your budget. By far the most obvious and important things to ask yourself are:

WHAT CAN I AFFORD?
As we all know in life, we can only have what we can afford.

The main elements that make up a self-build budget:

> **1 - The cost of purchasing your land including legal fees**
>
> **2 - Design costs**
>
> **3 - Infrastructure costs**
>
> **4 - Build costs**
>
> **5 - The cost of finance**

Some of these costs can be considered as a fixed cost, like the cost of your land and associated fees. Build costs and the cost of finance are far harder to quantify. Let's take all these elements that make up a budget individually.

1 - Costs of land and legal fees: This cost will pretty much always be a fixed cost. Once you have agreed the price of your land and you have negotiated a price for all associated fees, plus the cost of land registry, you will now have a figure that you can use while working out your budget.

2 - Design costs: This element of the budget is far harder to quantify as there is a lot of information to be collated to work out this portion of your budget.

If you're using an architects practice you can instruct them to collate all the information required plus prepare and submit all drawings to the relevant authorities. They will probably give you a price for carrying out this work.

Listed below is all the information that will be required to enable you to work out your design cost budget:

Planning application drawings
Planning fees
Building regulation drawings
Building regulation application fees plus inspection fees
Structural calculations
SAP calculations
EPC

A good architect practice should be able to give you a price for a complete package. It is not uncommon to re-design certain aspects of your development. This will inevitably incur an extra cost to your budget.

If you're going down the route of using a designer or CAD technician you will probably find he/she will only be able to produce your planning and working drawings; all the other information that you will require to successfully complete your project (as listed) you will have to obtain yourself.

3 - Infrastructure costs: There are many different things to be considered when trying to budget for infrastructure costs. Roads and sewers are normally the first things to consider when budgeting your infrastructure costs. Sometimes your infrastructure may be as simple as just having to pay for dropped kerbs and a connection into a existing mains sewer. Please note that any works to be carried out off-site must involve contact with the relevant authorities, i.e. highways and your local authority. It is not uncommon, as part of planning to have to add or re-site a lighting column. You will find all local authorities have a department that deals with street lighting and they will also give you a price for carrying out these works. When obtaining prices for works off-site make sure that any contractors that are pricing these works have street work permits in place. Your local authority will be able to provide you with a list of their approved street work contractors. You will only be able to use contractors that are on their list.

Another infrastructure expense will be the costs of incoming services to your property i.e. gas, water, electric and any media. You can use a multi-utility company who will give you a price to make all these connections, or you can ask for prices individually.

4 – Build costs: This is by far the most difficult part of quantifying your budget as there are many different aspects to take into consideration. Initially you must have some idea of how much money you will have available to spend on building your new property. This must be taken into consideration well before you start to have your property designed, as the design and materials used will almost certainly influence the budget.

Build ability is the keyword here, which basically means the simpler the design i.e. fewer corners, the cheaper the build costs will be. If you are planning a house which looks much grander in its design - maybe having bay windows, lower roofs and fancy porches, your build costs will be much higher. Once you have had your property designed in a manner that will suit your budget then you have to consider what materials are to be used internally and externally. Your next consideration whilst preparing your budget will be labour costs. If at all possible try to obtain a fixed price for labour, as paying day-rates makes it almost impossible to budget.

The most common way of budgeting build costs would be to employ a quantity surveyor (QS). He/she will then produce what is known as a bill of quantities; for a QS to produce a bill of quantities he will require full specifications of your requirements relating to the construction of your property. If there are any elements of your property that you have not already decided upon at this stage you will have to set a budget for these items, for example a kitchen, but you still need an idea of how much you are willing to spend on these items. These can then be added to a bill of quantities which is known as a PC sum. (PC being prime cost). The more information you can produce at the outset the more accurate your build costs budget will be.

Don't forget to consider things like patio areas, garden walls, fencing and driveways as part of your external works.

The proper procurement of materials will give you big savings throughout your project. The best way of saving money on the purchase of materials is by opening accounts at various builders' merchants. If you explain the size of your project and your material requirements they will be more than happy to give you prices for all your material requirements.

Some builders' merchants will offer you a service of quantifying all the material requirements in your build. This service is not normally free but if you then go on to use the merchant they will reimburse you for the cost of this service.

Negotiate
Always negotiate before purchasing any materials.

You will find large discounts can be achieved on most building products.

The labour element of your building budget is always a difficult task to quantify. When obtaining prices make sure you issue subcontractors with as much information as possible, as you will find all variations will have to be paid for. A lot of builders will charge heavily for variations.

Try to obtain prices regarding labour from reputable tradesmen; the cheapest price doesn't always give you the best job. It is usual to obtain three quotes for labour; however bricklayers will work on a price per thousand for laying bricks and a price per metre for laying blocks.

5 - Cost of finance: This directly relates to interest charges on all borrowed money and the duration that you will be requiring to borrow. The cost of finance can increase your overall budget by quite a considerable amount, so it is worth shopping around for your best finance package. Once you have collated all these elements of your budget and have added them together this will give you your budget for your project. However it is prudent to include an amount of money to cover any extra work that may be required, I would suggest a figure of about 10% for budgeting purposes.

Once you have produced your budget make sure it is affordable.

Incoming Services

Incoming Services to a new property is any utility or service that will be connected to your home and will have a supplier or shipper that will bill you for the use of the service provided.

These services will generally be:

Water

Gas

Electric

Media

When constructing a single dwelling you can usually gain access to the mains, where you will then be able to have a connection made to service your property.

If new mains have to be laid to accommodate your requirements this will significantly increase the cost of your project, plus it can also extend the length of time to complete your project.

Applying for services

There are two ways of applying for your services. You can apply for your services individually or you can use a multi utility provider. The advantage of using a multi-utility provider is that you only have one point of contact, compared with having to co-ordinate each individual service which may be required.

The route to follow for applying for services individually:

Gas
You have to apply to National Grid for all new gas supplies; they have qualifying criteria, as follows:

● The property is used mainly as a domestic private residence, i.e. house, flat, bungalow etc.

● You require a maximum of four new gas connections

- The property does not already have a live gas service

- The gas meter position will be no more than 3m above the ground, or on the first floor or below

- You have the name of the future gas consumer

- The land between where you want the meter and the property boundary is no more than 40 metres

- Your property boundary is no more than 23m from the mains in the street

- Your peak hourly gas use is below 295 kW per hour

If the National Grid has to extend a main, the National Grid will undertake a feasibility study to calculate the costs. For the project to proceed to the construction phase, 40% or greater of customers are required to agree and pay their premise contribution.

Information and considerations that National Grid will require when applying for a new supply:

You will be required to nominate a chosen gas supplier. For new build properties National Grid require scaled site plans and a ground location plan showing the new build property in relation to the road before they are able to progress with your order.

You will then be required to complete an online application form.

All new gas supplies require a new meter box, which is usually positioned externally. There are five different options: a built-in recessed box, a surface-mounted wall box, a semi-concealed in-ground box, a wall-mounted protruding kiosk or a freestanding kiosk.

You may have decided on a preferred position for your gas meter but be aware that not all positions are acceptable. This is due to a number of health and safety regulations which are important to consider. A new meter cannot be located more than 2m from the front of the property. Consideration should be given to the position of any manhole covers, all drains under this position and along the proposed route of the service pipe.

The position and installation of gas meters shall comply with the Gas Safety Regulations 1994 and BS 6400: 1997 specification installations of domestic gas meters.

Meter box locations that should be avoided:

Locations in close proximity to any source of heat or where they may be subjected to any extremes of temperature

Meters should not be sited within 300mm of the flue pipe from any gas appliances. Boiler rooms should also be avoided

Where food is stored or in bathrooms

Where it might be liable to damage or be causing an obstruction

Where it might be affected by a corrosive atmosphere

The meter must not be located where it will be in contact with cement or a floor that may be frequently wet

The meter shall be no closer than 150mm to an electricity meter.

Excavating
You only get the option of excavating for the service on your own land. National Grid will do all excavation works and reinstatement works of land off-site. If you require to pre-excavate a trench across your land, fill out your application form and indicate the section: *I will dig all holes and refill.* If you are excavating your own trench it must be to a depth of 425mm and must be between 200mm to

300 mm wide. The bottom of the trench must be level and free from all sharp stones and all stone materials which may damage the service pipe. In any ground containing sharp stones it will be necessary to excavate a further 75 mm and fill the space with a fine material, e.g. stone dust or sand, to lay the new pipe on. Cement-based materials must not be used as a fill material around the pipe.

The process of installing a new gas main in steps:

1 - Send a Request online. (National Grid will decide if any additional information is required and may require carrying out a site survey)

2 - When you have received your quote it must be paid for in full

3 - National Grid will contact you with a date for carrying out the work

4 - You will then have to contact your chosen gas supplier to have your meter fitted

Note
National Grid are not gas suppliers; they are there to maintain the infrastructure.

Water
You will have to apply for a new water supply via whoever your local water supplier is. This would be the same company that bills you for your water usage, for example Thames Water or United Utilities.

You will have to submit an application for a new supply. Some water companies send out their field engineers to assess and discuss your requirements on site. Other water companies require an application form filled out and sent online or by post.

Once you have established who your water supplier is you will find they will have plenty of guidance available to assist you successfully obtaining a new supply.

Listed are the usual costs and procedures involved when having a new water supply laid and connected.

Some suppliers charge you for providing a quote, but this charge is normally waived providing you accept the quote within 3 months.

You will be required to provide scaled drawings showing your boundary and your building entry point for your new water supply. Your water supplier will then be able to determine the best route which will normally be the nearest, to allow a connection to their existing mains.

There will be a service connection charge. You will be responsible for the excavation, supply and laying of the new main from your agreed boundary point to the entry point of your new property.

Most new water services are 25mm polyethylene. If when you are laying your new supply and there is contamination present in the ground, you will have to upgrade your new polyethylene pipe to make sure it is suitably protected.

The water supplier will quote for connecting your service pipe to their main and installing a water meter in an agreed position to your new property. They will re-instate all excavations outside your boundary; inside your boundary will be your responsibility.

Take note that the new water service when laid has to be inspected before it can be backfilled, unless you or your ground worker can provide a WIAPS certificate; the new water pipe should be to a depth not less than 750mm and no more than 1350mm. When backfilling your new water pipe you should cover the pipe with a fine fill approximately 150mm above the pipe and then lay a warning tape before completing the backfill.

There will be an infrastructure charge. This is a one-off payment which is charged on all new properties when they are connected for the first time.

You will also be charged a sewage and surface water infrastructure charge. This is also a one-off payment; be aware that your water supplier is also responsible for the discharge of rain water and sewerage relating to your property and charges will be levied accordingly.

Incoming Services

Building water charge – this is another one off charge for water used during the construction of a new dwelling. This cost is currently around £25. You will find that all new water connections are now metered.

Electricity

The electrical industry has three key stake holder areas. They are:

- Generators – Responsible for generating the electricity we use in our homes, they supply generated energy into the national transmission network and through to the regional distribution networks

- Distributors – The owners and operators of cables and pylons that bring electricity from the national transmission networks to homes and businesses

- Suppliers – The companies who supply and sell electricity to the consumer

When you require a new electric supply you will need to apply to your distributor as listed below. (**Distribution Network Operator (DNO) Companies**)

Area	Company	Emergency No.	General Enquiries No.
North Scotland	Scottish & Southern Energy	0800 300 999	0845 071 3954
South Scotland	Scottish Power	0845 272 7999	0845 273 4444
North East England	Northern Powergrid	0800 668 877	0845 070 7172
North West	Electricity North West Ltd	0800 195 4141	0800 048 1820
Yorkshire	Northern Powergrid	0800 375 675	0845 602 4453
East Midlands	Western Power Distribution	0800 056 8090	0800 096 3080
West Midlands	Western Power Distribution	0800 328 1111	0800 096 3080
Eastern England	UK Power Networks	0800 783 8838	0845 601 4516
South Wales	Western Power Distribution	0800 052 0400	0845 601 3341
Southern England	Scottish & Southern Energy	0800 072 7282	0845 071 3953
London	UK Power Networks	0800 028 0247	0845 601 4516
South East England	UK Power Networks	0800 783 8866	0845 601 4516
South West England	Western Power Distribution	0800 365 900	0845 601 2989
North Wales, Merseyside and Cheshire	Scottish Power	0845 272 2424	0845 273 4444

When applying for your new connection you will have to nominate a supplier. It will also be the responsibility of the supplier to install a meter to your property.

New connection process

You will need to complete an application for including your required electrical loadings; they will also require a scaled site plan indicating entry points to your new dwelling.

The distribution company will then register your project and produce a quotation.

You accept your quotation by completing and returning the following:

- Quote acceptance form
- VAT declaration (if relevant)
- Site information sheet
- A copy of your postal address as confirmed by your local Council
- Payment

You must then carry out your on-site works, which will be inspected to ensure you are ready to be connected.

You will then be notified of a connection date.

They will then come and make the connection.

You will then have to apply to your nominated supplier for them to come and fit a meter.

Ducting and Excavation

You will have to excavate to a depth of 450mm for a low voltage service and 600mm for a high voltage main.

You will have to purchase and lay all ducting and meter boxes.

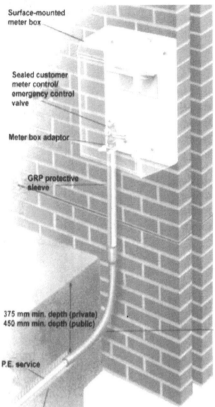

Surface-mounted meter box

Sealed customer meter control/ emergency control valve

Meter box adaptor

GRP protective sleeve

375 mm min. depth (private)
450 mm min. depth (public)

PVC preformed sleeve bend

P.E. service

A draw rope will be required in the duct.

As you are backfilling the trench you must put warning tape over the duct (usually 150mm). You must clearly mark the end of the duct.

You will be asked to supply an 'as laid' drawing clearly indicating the route of the duct. The route must be agreed with your distributor.

Your Meter

In order to obtain your meter, firstly you will need to appoint an electricity supplier. You will be required to provide a full council-approved postal address. Your distributor will have issued you with your MPAN (meter point administration number) which will be unique to your address. Your supplier will require this to enable them to book your meter to be fitted.

Media

Most properties have a BT connection; however there are now other choices available like cable TV or Virgin Media.

Prices and packages do vary but most media service providers will try to accommodate your requirements.

Meters
You cannot have a meter fitted until your supply has been installed and your internal wiring is complete.

If a BT land line is required, they will usually send one of their engineers to assess if the connection is to be overhead or underground, in which instance ducting will have to be laid. If ducting has to be laid they normally supply this to you free of charge although the laying of it will be down to you, which you will have to carry out to their requirements. They will also discuss entry points to your new dwelling.

BT has a one off connection charge for a new service. If you are taking out a broadband and TV package you may get this charge reduced. Virgin Media do offer free connection, but is not available in all areas.

Recommended arrangement of services under a 2 metre footpath indicating depths and distances and relative positioning.

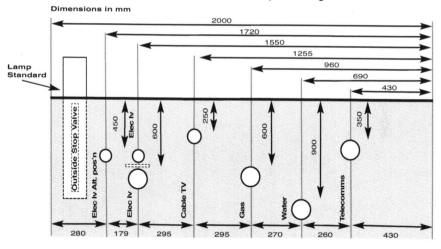

Multi-Utility Provider You may wish to use a multi-utility provider. You will still have to meet the same criteria regarding your commitment to the on-site works, but the big advantage is that you will only have to deal with one point of contact, as they will programme and connect your services (Gas, Water and Electric. Media will still be for you to arrange).

Multi Utility companies are more suited for developers with sites of multiple houses rather than one-off developments.

BUILD YOUR OWN
HOUSE

Your choice of materials will have a huge impact on your project in both appearance, personal choice and budget.

Listed are the major points to be considered before purchasing materials:

- Cost
- Local Authority Planning Department or conservation approval
- Suitability for the design of your new home
- Material schedule
- Availability

Costs –
Materials can be categorised into groups
General building materials
Finishing and decorative materials

General Building - Materials are for example blocks, bricks, concrete etc. You will also be purchasing materials for finishing, for example wall tiles, light fittings, kitchen units etc.

Let's consider general building materials first. A lot of building materials are used in the construction of a house. Providing they fit in with the design to be used in your project, they can be purchased from whoever is going to give you the best price.

Your best approach would be to contact various builders' merchants to gain your best price. You certainly don't have to feel embarrassed about doing this, as no builder expects to pay the marked up price for materials. A 50% to 75% discount off list prices is not unusual on some products. So you can see how important it is to always negotiate the best price. Alternatively you may wish to search for materials online.

Finishing and Decorative materials - An area where it is easy to let your budget run away with you. If possible try to keep within your original budget when purchasing items like kitchens and wall tiles. This is not always easy as you are

likely to see something that you consider to be a bit nicer than what you originally budgeted for. For example you can purchase a kitchen for just a few thousand pounds or perhaps you want that top of the range one that can run into many thousands of pounds. You must try to stay within the price range of what you originally budgeted for. Spending that extra bit of money here and there can soon add up to a lot of money that you may not have budgeted for.

Local Authority Planning Department or conservation approval - Before you purchase any materials ensure there are no planning or conservation conditions, which stipulate that certain types of materials have to be used. It is not uncommon for planning authorities to request material samples to be approved. This would normally relate to external wall finishes, roof coverings and windows. This all depends on the area you live in and local conservation policies.

Suitable for the design of your new home - The design of all construction materials will have to meet certain technical requirements. If you are unsure if a material is suitable for use in the construction of your new property, ask your designer, architect or building control officer for guidance.

Never purchase construction materials until you are certain that they are fit for use within the construction of your new property. Most of the information you require regarding material suitability can be found on your building regulation drawings.

Material Schedule - It is always good to produce a material schedule, which would normally include the following:

> *-The length of time required by the supplier from when an order is placed to when it is likely to be delivered. This period is often referred to as a lead time*

> *-The date you require the material to be ordered*

> *-Actual date ordered*

> *-Date material is delivered to site*

Materials

Example of a Material Schedule

Material	Lead Time	Date Required	Order date	Delivered to Site
Concrete	3 days			
Bricks	4 weeks			
Blocks	1 week			
Lintels	2 weeks			
Wall insulation	1 week			
Window former	2 weeks			
Floor joists	3 weeks			
Roof Trusses	4 weeks			
Roof tiles	3 weeks			
Windows	5 weeks			
Stairs	3 weeks			
Studwork	2 days			
Door casings	3 days			
Window boards	1 week			
Plasterboard	8 days			
External Doors	5 weeks			
Internal Doors	2 weeks			
Kitchen	6 weeks			
Sanitary ware	3 weeks			
Wall Tiles	1 week			
Door Furniture	2 days			

This is only an example, but it allows you to build up a picture of what materials you require and when you need them delivered to site. You should always aim to have your materials delivered to site when they are required to be installed or used; this is called just in time ordering within the construction industry. It also ensures that materials are not delivered too early, where they run the risk of being damaged. You also don't want to have to pay for materials until they are needed.

You can modify a material schedule to suit your own project, as all projects will differ from one another.

Availability

This is a key consideration; it is always worth checking the availability of materials against the quantities required.

For example: a merchant may have your required brick type in stock, but he may not have the quantity you require. Also make sure they are not a discontinued line.

If at all possible it is always a good idea to allocate an area where you can store materials on site before they are required; this should prevent materials getting damaged. Most materials come with instructions on how best to store prior to being used.

Some building products now come with **COSHH** information, which stands for Control of Substances Hazardous to Health. This information will make you aware of any health risks relating to the product and preventative measures that should be taken.

Having a pre-prepared Construction Programme is of vital importance to the success of any project.

Time Scale
Remember, if you don't know the time scale for completing your project, there is little chance anyone else will!

If you visit any construction site office of a main building contractor, you will almost certainly see a construction programme pinned up on the wall. Without one there is little chance of successfully completing a project on time, within budget and in an organised manner. Good programming is always a key to the successful outcome of a project.

There are many things to consider when producing a construction programme, bearing in mind elements of your construction project that will be unique to you and will affect time scales.

Construction Programme considerations

Start date – you cannot set a start date until you have put many aspects of your project in place. The 10 previous chapters of information cover all the important areas in that respect.

Key consideration check list

- Planning Permission is approved with any outstanding conditions being dealt with accordingly

- You have all your building regulation drawings approved

- You know the total cost of your project and you have your finance in place

- You are building in accordance with the sustainable code for dwellings

- All warranties are in place

- Required incoming services have been determined and applied for

Producing A Construction Programme

- You have decided upon materials that are to be used for your project and you have produced a material schedule.

Once you have determined a start date and have an idea of the duration of your project, you will then be ready to produce your construction programme.

It is up to the individual how detailed the construction programme will be, but it should always include key operations along with their time scales.

Time scales will be determined by the size of your property, along with the size of the labour force you are going to employ.

Depending on your project you should be able to adapt a programme to suit your own requirements, detailing it accordingly. Your construction programme needs to be used in conjunction with your material schedule.

Construction programmes should be used as a tool and updated weekly, as it is not uncommon for delays.

Common reasons you may encounter delays:

- Inclement weather

- Being let down with material deliveries

- Labour issues

- Design changes to your project

There will undoubtedly be many reasons that you may need to revise or update a construction programme, but it is of vital importance that you keep it as up to date as practicably possible.

11

Producing A Construction Programme

The following table is an example of Construction Programme for a brick built dwelling of 1,000sq ft.

Operation/Task	1	2	3	4	5	6	7	8	9	10	11	12	13	14	15	16	17	18	19	20	21	22	23	24	25
Site prep	X																								
Foundation		X																							
Footings to DPC			X																						
Slab				X																					
Drainage					X																				
1st lift brickwork						X	X																		
Joists								X																	
Wall Plate								X	X																
Main roof										X	X														
Windows												X													
1st fix joiner														X											
1st fix plumber														X											
1st fix electrician														X											
Plasterer																X	X								
2nd fix joiner																		X							
2nd fix plumber																			X						
2nd fix electrician																			X						
Fit kitchen																				X					
Wall Tiler																					X				
Painter																						X	X		
Mastic pointing																								X	
Commission																								X	
Snag/Clean																								X	
Snag/Clean																									X
External works																X	X	X	X	X	X	X	X		

The X indicates when tasks or operations are to take place

Enabling Works, also referred to as site preparation. This should take place prior to the commencement of construction work to your new property.

There are many things that should be taken into consideration when preparing your site ready for construction.

Access – You must consider all access routes on and off your site, taking into consideration the size and weight of the vehicles that will be making deliveries. This may require constructing temporary roads. Temporary roads can be as simple as just laying clean stone and then compacting. When considering access also take into consideration routes for your delivery vehicles, for example: make a note and try to avoid roads with weight restrictions or low bridges.

Site Parking – If at all possible allocated parking for site workers is ideal. However on a small site this isn't always possible, so you should look at other alternatives, like nearby car parks or getting permission to park in areas that are in close proximity to your site. Try not to allow your workforce to just turn up and abandon their vehicles where they see fit, as you will soon be spending much of your time acting as a traffic warden.

Fencing – You will need to fence off your site prior to construction, as you do not want to have the general public wandering onto your site without permission. Fencing also acts as security for your materials and also prevents the public accessing your site where there is a potential that they could be harmed. If possible you should consider erecting fencing or building walls that are going to be a permanent fixture, as this is the most cost-effective approach. If this is not possible then you should erect some temporary security fencing. This should be of a height of at least 1.8m.

Signage – Signage should be attached to your fencing or placed so it is clearly visible, making the general public aware that they are entering a building site and warning of any potential dangers.

Enabling Works

Your Neighbours – It is always a good idea to inform any neighbours of your intentions, explaining that you will be having many deliveries, informing them of your time period, and making them aware there may be activities that will cause an element of noise. It is also a chance for them to voice any concerns, especially if you are building near a school or a hospital. You should avoid blocking any access that may be required by your neighbours.

Emergency Services – You should always make sure you give clear access to your site and your neighbours in case the emergency services need to be called.

Storage of materials – If at all possible you should set aside an area where you can store your building materials. You should try to allocate an area that is accessible from the road to enable deliveries of bricks, blocks, timber etc. You will have to ensure you have the means to cover any perishable items or items that can be affected by the elements.

Temporary services – You will almost certainly require electricity and a water supply to your site. You can apply for temporary mains services, but this can be costly and you would normally only do this if you were building multiple dwellings. Generators are the quickest and easiest ways to generate power to a building site.

There are many companies that will hire or sell you a generator which is suitable for site use. See if you can get a temporary water supply from a neighbouring building. Alternatively, you can apply for a licence that will enable you to use a nearby hydrant. You may have to consider a water bowser; you can hire a bowser that can be towed.

Toilet and washing facilities – You will have to provide a toilet and hand washing facilities for your site operatives. The quickest and easiest way to do this would be to hire a Portable Toilet; they usually have a hand wash basin incorporated in them. Most hire companies, as part of the hire terms, will come and service these at agreed intervals, usually weekly. Once you have taken all these points into consideration and have completed any work that you deem to be appropriate you will be ready to commence construction of your new dwelling.

Site Setting Out is ensuring that your new dwelling, including any boundary walls, fencing, drainage and driveways, are all positioned correctly, in accordance with your planning approval.

Note ! *It is of the upmost importance that your new dwelling, including boundaries, is set out in accordance with your planning permission. New structures have in the past had enforcement action taken against them where they have been positioned incorrectly and as a result have had to be demolished.*

The most common approach to setting out a dwelling would be to employ a Setting Out engineer. Setting Out engineers will position your dwelling correctly using instrumentation combined with National Grid and Ordnance Survey co-ordinates. They will accurately, by physical means, precisely set out the dwelling onto the ground.

They will normally set up a series of profiles with nails inset into the top to allow for strings to be attached from one to another. Engineers generally set houses out to the outside face of the brick or blockwork. They will give you as many points as you require. The shape of your new dwelling will dictate how many profiles are set up.

It is a good idea to have profiles off-set, out of the way, so they can still be used after the foundations have been excavated, for the setting out of brick or blockwork. This will save the engineer having to revisit the site, saving you money.

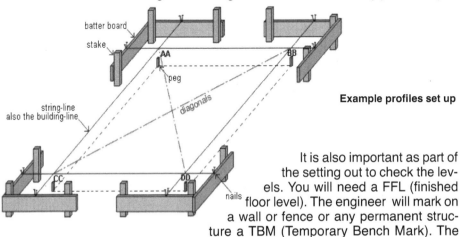

Example profiles set up

It is also important as part of the setting out to check the levels. You will need a FFL (finished floor level). The engineer will mark on a wall or fence or any permanent structure a TBM (Temporary Bench Mark). The TBM will have a value which can used in conjunction with any other levels you may require while constructing your new property.

12.C
Foundations

Foundations are designed to take into account ground conditions, the vicinity of trees and the structure that is to be constructed on top of them. This information is then collated and a design is based on these findings.

Structural Engineers carry out foundation designs. When a foundation has been designed it needs to be submitted for approval to building control and your warranty provider.

If for any reason once constructed your foundations fail, providing you have constructed them as designed, a claim can be made against the structural engineer's indemnity insurance.

Design
Always have your Foundation Plans designed by a qualified Structural Engineer.

So it is of utmost importance to follow the design and methods of constructing your foundations.

If designs and methods of construction have been followed it is extremely rare that a foundation will fail.

Listed are the main considerations and methodology of designing foundations:

1 – Ground Conditions

2 – Building near trees

3 – The type of foundation best suited to your project

The objective of these considerations is to ensure that your site is properly assessed and investigated, to ensure the foundation design is best suited to your project and any remediation, if necessary, is carried out prior to the construction of your foundations.

The main foundation considerations in more detail, which should enable you to successfully design and construct your foundations:

Ground conditions

An initial assessment will have to be carried out comprising a desk top study, which is a collection of information that is historically available. This would include the site and the vicinity, answering questions such as:

Has the site been previously used for tipping or landfill?
Are there any known mining works?
Was the site previously used for industrial or commercial use?
Has it previously been farmed?

There are various sources that can be used to determine this information such as:

Ordnance Survey
Local Historic Records and Government Offices
British Geological Survey
Environment Agency
Soil Survey Maps
National Coal Board

With the next process of your initial assessment you need to conduct a walk over survey. This is a first-hand inspection of your site where the following considerations will be made:

Topography -
Features to be taken into account would be:

Is the site sloping?
Is there evidence of tipped material?
Is the site at the bottom of a valley?
Has the site any signs of subsidence?
Are there any signs of landslip?

Surface and Ground water -
Has the site previously flooded?
Is the land waterlogged?
Are there any springs, ditches, ponds or water courses present?

Ground description -
Is there is evidence of cracking? This may indicate a shrinkable sub-soil.
Is there any evidence of peat?
Is there a mixture of the type of ground? For example sand and clay.

Structural Evidence -
Is there evidence of any structural movement to nearby properties?

Trees and Vegetation -
Note species of any trees that may be present, along with their height
Are there any hedges present?
Is there any evidence of former hedges or trees?

Once all the results of the initial assessment have been recorded they will need to be evaluated by a consultant or specialist.

A site where hazards are not suspected requires a basic investigation carried out. This would also be done by a consultant or specialist and would include:

Basic Geotechnical Investigation - This includes digging trial pits (in some instances boreholes may be required). The number of trial pits or boreholes will depend on the consistency of the soil and geology across the site.

Sampling and testing of material taken from trial pits or boreholes should be undertaken; this will indicate any contamination that may be present.

Detailed Investigation - A detailed investigation will be carried out if any hazards are suspected as identified from an initial and basic investigation.

Detailed investigations should include:
- Taking into consideration the site and the adjacent area
- Surface and ground water conditions
- The nature of the soil
- The site geology
- Previous use of the site
- Possible presence of gas in the ground. If it is determined that gas is present then a full gas investigation should be carried out, which must include flow measurements.

All factual data obtained from the detailed investigation should then be presented in a way to enable foundations to be designed taking into account all identified hazards.

Site Remediation may be required before you can proceed with your foundations.

Remediation techniques -
- Consider changing layout to isolate any potential hazards.
- Remove contaminates by excavation. (All contaminated waste has to be transported to a specified and licenced tip. All documentation must be kept).
- Install ground barriers.
- Cover and cap contaminated area.
- Stabilise ground by using biological or chemical means.

All information should be assessed by a consultant or specialist who is acceptable to your warranty provider.

Building near trees -
Trees, hedgerows and shrubs take moisture from the ground. In cohesive soils such as clay significant changes to moisture content causes ground movement. In order to minimise this risk foundations should be designed to accommodate any ground movement. The removal of existing trees will also have an impact on ground movement. Sub soils like clay are extremely shrinkable causing ground movement, which is referred to as Heave. Foundations should always accommodate Heave.

TRENCH FOUNDATION WITH CLAY BOARD

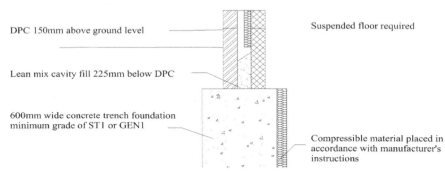

DPC 150mm above ground level

Suspended floor required

Lean mix cavity fill 225mm below DPC

600mm wide concrete trench foundation minimum grade of ST1 or GEN1

Compressible material placed in accordance with manufacturer's instructions

In these instances Clay Board, which is a compressible material, is often introduced. The following chart indicates foundations depths when building near trees. It is important that you correctly identify the species of the tree and record the height.

Species	Distance from Building												
	1m	2m	4m	6m	8m	10m	12m	14m	16m	18m	20m	22m	24m
English Oak	*	*	*	2.50	2.15	1.95	1.80	1.65	1.45	1.30	1.10	0.95	0.90
Black Poplar	*	*	2.50	2.40	2.25	2.15	2.00	1.90	1.70	1.60	1.45	1.30	1.20
Weeping Willow	*	*	2.50	2.40	1.95	1.85	1.55	1.40	1.20	0.95			
Hawthorn	*	2.40	2.10	1.75	1.45	1.00							
Leylandii	*	*	*	2.25	2.10	1.95	1.75	1.60	1.40	1.25	1.15	0.90	
Cedar	1.65	1.50	1.20	0.90									
Douglas Fir	1.65	1.50	1.20	0.90									
Pine	1.65	1.50	1.20	0.90									
Spruce	1.65	1.50	1.20	0.90									
Chestnut	1.70	1.60	1.45	1.30	1.20	1.10	0.90						
Ash	1.75	1.65	1.50	1.40	1.30	1.15	1.00						
Lime	1.75	1.65	1.50	1.40	1.30	1.15	1.00						
Sycamore	1.75	1.65	1.50	1.40	1.30	1.15	1.00						
Pear	1.65	1.60	1.30	1.05									
Cherry	1.75	1.65	1.50	1.30	1.15	1.00							
Alder	1.70	1.60	1.45	1.30	1.20	0.90							
Maple	1.70	1.60	1.45	1.30	1.20	0.90							
Beech	1.70	1.60	1.45	1.30	1.20	0.90							
Plum	1.65	1.50	1.20	0.90									
Laurel	1.65	1.50	1.20	0.90									
Apple	1.65	1.50	1.20	0.90									
Laburnum	1.15	1.05	0.90										
Birch	1.20	1.10	0.95										
Holly	1.20	1.10	0.95										
Magnolia	1.10	1.00											
Mulberry	1.10	1.00											

Foundation Depth in Metres

The type of Foundation best suited to your project

Strip and Trench fill foundations are the most common and usually the most cost effective foundation design. If hazardous ground conditions have been identified then you may have to consider an alternative foundation design. This could be a Raft or Piling. All load-bearing elements of your project should be adequately supported by foundations.

Elements requiring foundations include the following:
- External wall ● Internal load-bearing walls ● Separating (party) walls
- Chimney breasts ● Piers ● Garden walls

STRIP FOUNDATION
Strip and Trench fill foundations

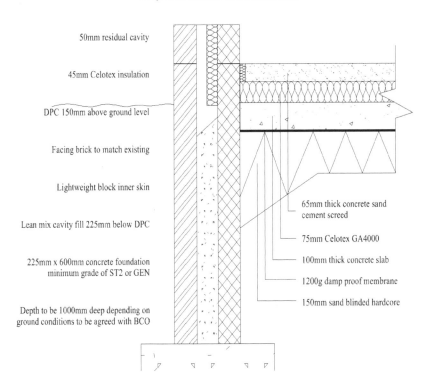

50mm residual cavity

45mm Celotex insulation

DPC 150mm above ground level

Facing brick to match existing

Lightweight block inner skin

Lean mix cavity fill 225mm below DPC

225mm x 600mm concrete foundation minimum grade of ST2 or GEN

Depth to be 1000mm deep depending on ground conditions to be agreed with BCO

65mm thick concrete sand cement screed

75mm Celotex GA4000

100mm thick concrete slab

1200g damp proof membrane

150mm sand blinded hardcore

TRENCH FOUNDATION

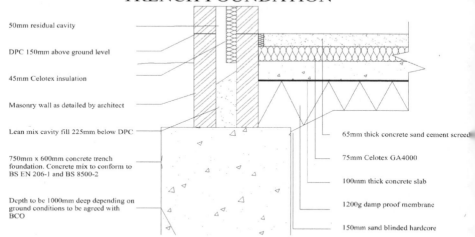

50mm residual cavity

DPC 150mm above ground level

45mm Celotex insulation

Masonry wall as detailed by architect

Lean mix cavity fill 225mm below DPC

750mm x 600mm concrete trench foundation. Concrete mix to conform to BS EN 206-1 and BS 8500-2

Depth to be 1000mm deep depending on ground conditions to be agreed with BCO

65mm thick concrete sand cement screed

75mm Celotex GA4000

100mm thick concrete slab

1200g damp proof membrane

150mm sand blinded hardcore

To avoid frost, the depth to the underside of a foundation should be a minimum of 450mm below finished ground level. When excavating strip foundations the following should be considered: foundation depths should be adequate for site conditions; in shrinkable soil your consultant may need to refer to a plasticity index to determine a suitable foundation design. Foundations should always have a clean and firm bearing. Where these are to be stepped, the height of the step should not exceed the thickness of the foundation.

STEP FOR STRIP FOUNDATION

Stepped foundations should over lap by twice the height of the step, by the thickness of the foundations, or 300mm whichever is the greater

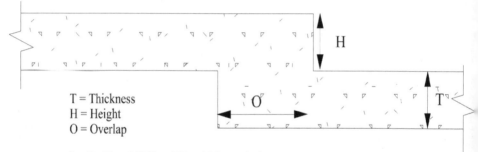

H

T = Thickness
H = Height
O = Overlap

O

T

O = 2 x H or 1 X T or 300, whichever is the greater

- Allow the foundation design to take into account any drainage or services
- You may need to accommodate existing services or drainage
- Always use the concrete mix that has been specified for your foundation design
- Reinforcing maybe required if you encounter small localised soft spots in your trenches
- When setting out your foundations ensure your walls will sit centrally on them
- If when excavating your foundations you encounter an unexpected change in ground conditions, you will have to refer the information back to your designer and the foundations may need to be modified accordingly.
- If roots are encountered while excavating you may need to excavate deeper
- The bottom of your trench should be compact, reasonably dry and even
- Services and drainage should not pass through the concrete of a strip foundation
- The concreting of strip foundations should be carried out as one continuous pour
- You should pour your foundation as soon as possible after they have been inspected

Alternative Foundations

Raft Foundation- A raft foundation is where the foundation is incorporated into the floor slab. Reinforcing is nearly always introduced where this type of foundation is used.

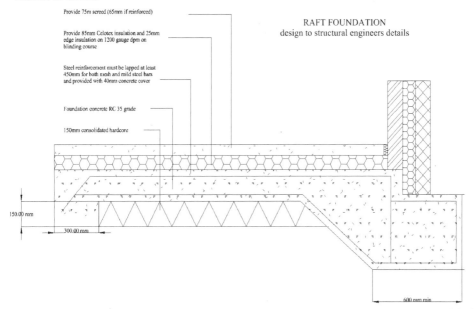

Provide 75m screed (65mm if reinforced)

Provide 85mm Celotex insulation and 25mm edge insulation on 1200 gauge dpm on blinding course

Steel reinforcement must be lapped at least 450mm for both mesh and mild steel bars and provided with 40mm concrete cover

Foundation concrete RC 35 grade

150mm consolidated hardcore

RAFT FOUNDATION
design to structural engineers details

150.00 mm

300.00 mm

600 mm min

Raft foundations must be constructed in accordance with the design. All required reinforcement shall be cut, bent and placed as shown in the design and should be concreted in one continuous pour.

Piled Foundations

There are many different piling techniques; piling is generally an expensive operation, especially as a one off. Apart from the piling operation you will also have to pay for the cost of mobilisation of a rig. Listed are some types of piled foundations that may be considered:

Piled Foundations

There are many variations and techniques for piled foundations. They are mostly designed and constructed by specialist contractors.

- Driven piles.
- Case driven piles.
- Stone Vibro piles.

After a piling operation has been completed, you will need to place ground beams on top of the piles. These can be either precast concrete beams or you will have to shutter and pour ground beams. Ground beams will be designed accordingly and all design information should be followed, including reinforcement. Block and brickwork can then be built on top of the ground beams.

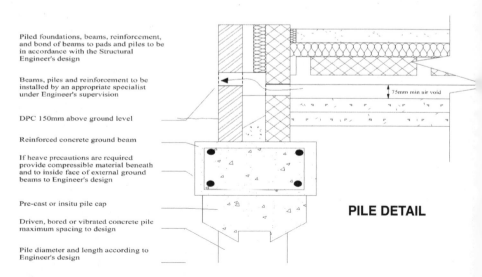

Piled foundations, beams, reinforcement, and bond of beams to pads and piles to be in accordance with the Structural Engineer's design

Beams, piles and reinforcement to be installed by an appropriate specialist under Engineer's supervision

DPC 150mm above ground level

Reinforced concrete ground beam

If heave precautions are required provide compressible material beneath and to inside face of external ground beams to Engineer's design

Pre-cast or insitu pile cap

Driven, bored or vibrated concrete pile maximum spacing to design

Pile diameter and length according to Engineer's design

75mm min air void

PILE DETAIL

Drainage (below ground)

Below ground drainage is split into two systems:-
Surface Water drainage and **Foul Water drainage.**

Surface water – Water that falls as rain or snow
Foul Water – Water which is produced as a waste product, for example bath water, washing-up water or water from flushing a toilet.

The two systems are designed separately. Foul water is directed to an outfall to allow it to be treated as it will be contaminated, whereas surface water is often discharged directly into existing water courses. This is not always the case; it is still common that offsite connections may be a combined system. However you will be required to design and lay two different systems on site before connecting to a combined outfall. This is for two main reasons, one is to prevent foul smells coming from any gullies that may be connected to your surface water system and secondly, in the future two separate mains systems may be required.

Note that if you are to use a combined system then the two systems must combine at the last manhole before leaving site.

Drainage Design
The following information that should be included in a drainage design:

- Clearly indicate which is surface water and which is foul water

  drainage (normally denoted on drawings as F for foul and S for Surface)
- The full proposed drainage layout
- Invert levels of proposed drainage
- Finished floor levels of new dwelling
- External finished levels
- Position of any proposed soakaways
- Position of any proposed water treatment plant that may need to be

  installed.

BUILD YOUR OWN
HOUSE

- Invert levels and locations of any existing drainage
- The diameter of pipes that are to be used
- The size and location of manholes and inspection chambers

All drainage schemes need to be approved by Local Building Control prior to them being laid. They must include all outfalls.

Surface Water Drainage: If you are unable to connect your surface water into an existing mains outfall or a water course, you will have to consider constructing a soakaway on site.

Surface Water Soakaway Design: Since April 2002, building regulations have required that there are sufficient arrangements to ensure surface water soakaways are effective.

Building Regulations H3 states:
'The requirements of H3 will be met if rainwater soaking into the ground is distributed sufficiently so that it does not damage foundations of the proposed buildings or adjacent structures'.

Soakaways must be able to store immediate storm-water run off and allow for the waters efficient infiltration into the adjacent soil. The time taken for efficient infiltration is used to determine the size of the soakaway required. Traditionally soakaways are square pits filled with rubble topped with a plastic membrane so as to prevent soil infiltration. This type of construction is still considered suitable in the majority of cases where serving areas less than 100m2, subject to the percolation test results and precise storage capacity calculations.
The three determining factors for soakaways are:-

1 - Position of the water table
2 - The size of the area to be drained
3 - The percolation rate of the soil/sub-soil
4 - Positioning of a soakaway

SOAKAWAY

Soakaway size and type dependent on
space requirements, site layout,
topography, water table, subsoil type, etc.
Designed to BS EN 752

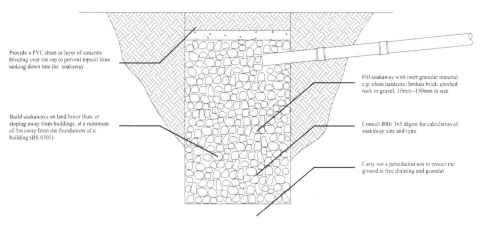

Provide a PVC sheet or layer of concrete blinding over the top to prevent topsoil from sinking down into the soakaway

Build soakaways on land lower than, or sloping away from buildings, at a minimum of 5m away from the foundations of a building (BS 8301)

Fill soakaway with inert granular material, e.g. clean hardcore, broken brick, crushed rock or gravel, 10mm -150mm in size

Consult BRE 365 digest for calculation of soakaway size and type

Carry out a percolation test to ensure the ground is free draining and granular

The Position of the water table

This is the first consideration when chosing a suitable site for a soakaway. It is common that a water table rises during the wet months and falls during the drier ones. If a site becomes waterlogged where the water table is exceptionally high then a soakaway may not function and an alternative method of displacing surface water may be required. It would be best if the bottom of an excavated soakaway is above the water table.

Area to be drained

The second consideration is to determine the size of the area that is to be drained, expressed in square metres. The area should include all roof areas and any impervious areas i.e. parking areas, patio areas and access paths.

Percolation tests

Percolation tests should be undertaken to determine the subsoil drainage capabilities. Next is the procedure for carrying out and recording percolation tests:

Percolation Test Method for Rain Water Disposal.

A hole 300mm square should be excavated to a depth 300mm below the proposed invert level of the incoming pipe. Where deep drains are necessary, the hole should conform to this shape at the bottom, but may be enlarged above the 300mm level to enable safe excavation to be carried out. Where very deep excavations are necessary, you should seek specialist advice. Fill the 300mm square section of the hole to a depth of at least 300mm with water and allow it to seep away overnight.

Next day, refill the 300mm square section of the hole with water to a depth of at least 300mm and observe the time, in seconds, for the water to seep away from 75% full to 25% full level (i.e. a depth of 150mm). Divide this time by 150mm. The answer gives the average time in seconds (Vp) required for the water to drop 1mm. For example 60mins divided by 150mm = 24 seconds (Vp = 24 seconds).

The test should preferably be carried out at least three times with at least two trial holes. The average figure from the tests should be taken. The test should not be carried out during abnormal weather conditions such as heavy rain, severe frost or drought. .

Where the test is carried out as described above, the soil infiltration rate (f) is related to the value (Vp) derived from the test by the equation: Formula to calculate the Soil Filtration rate:

f= 10-3
2Vp

The storage volume should then be calculated so that, over the duration the storm, the storage volume is sufficient to contain the difference between the inflow volume and the outflow volume. The inflow volume is calculated from the rainfall depth and the area drained. The outflow volume (O) is calculated from the equation:

O = as50 x f x D

Where as 50 is the area of the side of the storage volume when filled to 50% of its effective depth (for example (1m2/2) x 4 = 2m2) and (D) is the duration of the storm in minutes (for example 5 minutes).

Example:
Drained area
= 25m2

Incoming water
is 25m2 area x 10mm of rainfall = 0.25m3 of water to be disposed of.

Outflow volume
is: O = as50 x f x D therefore O = 2x 0.0002 x 5 and thus O = 0.002m3

Therefore required capacity is 0.25m3 - 0.002m3 = 0.248m3. Which means that a traditional rubble-filled soakaway measuring 1m3 below the inlet pipe and with, say, 20% void, ie 0.2m3 storage capacity, will not be adequate and the soakaway volume should be increased to 1.24m3 capacity.

Positioning of Soakaways
Soakaways should be positioned a minimum of 5 metres from any building (including buildings located beyond the boundary). The soakaway must be positioned lower than the area that is to be drained.

Foul Water Drainage
Where possible always consider connecting your foul water drainage into an existing main. You will have to apply to your utility provider if a new connection is required. If there isn't a mains sewer available for a connection then you will have to consider an alternative approach.

A sewage treatment plant would be the usual choice where a mains sewer connection cannot be achieved.

Sewage treatment is a process of removing contaminants from wastewater and household sewage. Its objective is to produce an environmentally safe fluid that can be safely reintroduced into a water course, or soakaway. There are many variations of sewage treatment plants on the market. The size will vary depending on the amount of properties and people that will be using the system.

Drainage

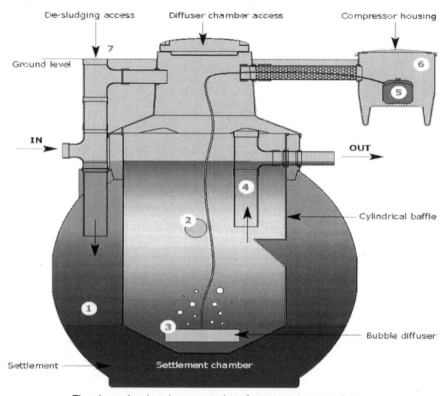

De-sludging access   Diffuser chamber access   Compressor housing

7

Ground level

IN

OUT

Cylindrical baffle

Bubble diffuser

Settlement   Settlement chamber

The above drawing shows a section of a water treatment plant

(1) Shows where the initial settlement takes place, with the heaviest solids sinking and the floating matter rising. The liquor from the main section is then transferred to the central chamber (2) where it is continuously aerated by the fine bubble diffuser (3) which encourages bacteria to provide the second stage of treatment. The mid-section of this treated effluent is then removed from the chamber through a calming pipe which allows a further brief settlement before discharge (4). The air compressor (5) and (6) runs continuously. (7) Point of access for desludging which is generally carried out annually.

If it is your intention for the treated fluid to be dispersed into a soakaway, a percolation test will be required to enable a suitable soakaway design.

- *A percolation test hole 300mm x 300mm x 300mm deep should be excavated below the proposed invert level of the effluent distribution pipe. For most sewage treatment units this depth is from 700mm down to 1 metre, i.e the base of the percolation test hole below is 1 metre below ground. This usually requires a large hole to be dug to stand in whilst digging the small percolation test hole.*

- *6 inch nails pushed into the sides of the hole, mark the hole 75mm from the bottom and 75mm from the top of the percolation test hole.*

- Fill the percolation test hole to a depth of at least 300mm with water and allow it to seep away overnight.

- Next day, refill the test hole with water to a depth of at least 300mm and see the time, in seconds, for the water to seep away from 75% full to 25% full level (i.e., a depth of 150mm). Divide this time by 150mm. The answer gives the average time in seconds (Vp) required for the water to drop 1mm.

- The percolation test should be carried out at least three times with at least three trial holes. The average figure from the tests should be taken. The test should not be carried out during abnormal weather conditions such as heavy rain, severe frost or drought.

- Drainage field soakaway disposal should only be used when percolation tests show average values of Vp of between 15 and 100 and the preliminary site assessment report and trial hole tests have been favourable. This minimum value ensures that untreated effluent can not percolate too rapidly into ground water. Where Vp is outside these limits effective disposal is unlikely to take place in a soakaway drainage field.

The percolation test calculations for a soakaway are as follows;

Area (A) = V X P X 0.20 for sewage treatment units and

Area (A) = V X P X 0.25 for septic tanks

V = the time is in seconds for the water in the test hole to drop by 1mm.

P = the max. number of persons that the unit is designed to serve

The calculation gives the AREA in SQUARE METRES required for the soakaway trenches. Further calculations are required to give the length of pipes required depending on the width of the trench, e.g. for a 600mm wide trench, the AREA would be divided by 0.6.

Soakaway drains **MUST NOT** be installed unless the Site Assessment and Soil Profile deep test hole show that there is a minimum of 1.2 metres between the bottom of the drain and the water table or bedrock. If it is less than this, then the water has not got enough soil depth to drain away.

Installing underground Drainage and Manhole construction

You must be able to access all sections of underground drainage be means of manholes, inspection chambers and rodding eyes and all drainage should be designed accordingly. Always lay drainage to the correct gradients, invert levels can normally be found on your drainage layout drawings. Too steep or too shallow drainage is likely to cause blockages. If you find there is a sudden change in levels whilst laying your drainage you will need to install a backdrop manhole. The drop-pipe can be either inside or outside the manhole, although it is more usual to have the drop-pipe on the outside.

BACKDROP MANHOLE WITH THE DROP
OUTSIDE THE MANHOLE
General guide only consult BS EN 1917 for more
details

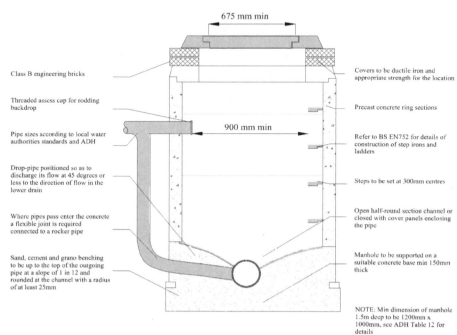

675 mm min

Class B engineering bricks

Threaded assess cap for rodding backdrop

Pipe sizes according to local water authorities standards and ADH

Drop-pipe positioned so as to discharge its flow at 45 degrees or less to the direction of flow in the lower drain

Where pipes pass enter the concrete a flexible joint is required connected to a rocker pipe

Sand, cement and grano benching to be up to the top of the outgoing pipe at a slope of 1 in 12 and rounded at the channel with a radius of at least 25mm

900 mm min

Covers to be ductile iron and appropriate strength for the location

Precast concrete ring sections

Refer to BS EN752 for details of construction of step irons and ladders

Steps to be set at 300mm centres

Open half-round section channel or closed with cover panels enclosing the pipe

Manhole to be supported on a suitable concrete base min 150mm thick

NOTE: Min dimension of manhole 1.5m deep to be 1200mm x 1000mm, see ADH Table 12 for details

Today, domestic properties have manholes which are preformed UPVC units. These are quick and easy to install. However you may need to brick-build a manhole if the manhole is in an area that will be used for heavy traffic. Once you have laid your drainage you will need to have it inspected before you are able to backfill.

BRICK BUILT MANHOLE

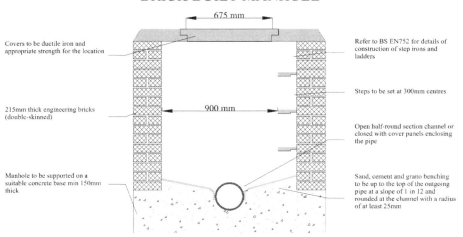

675 mm

Covers to be ductile iron and appropriate strength for the location

Refer to BS EN752 for details of construction of step irons and ladders

Steps to be set at 300mm centres

215mm thick engineering bricks (double-skinned)

900 mm

Open half-round section channel or closed with cover panels enclosing the pipe

Manhole to be supported on a suitable concrete base min 150mm thick

Sand, cement and grano benching to be up to the top of the outgoing pipe at a slope of 1 in 12 and rounded at the channel with a radius of at least 25mm

COVERS FOR DRAINAGE PIPES

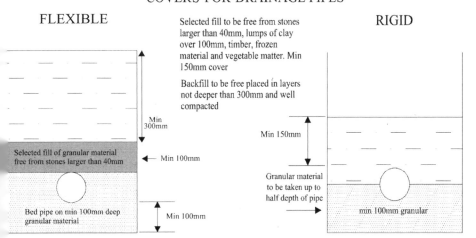

FLEXIBLE

Selected fill to be free from stones larger than 40mm, lumps of clay over 100mm, timber, frozen material and vegetable matter. Min 150mm cover

RIGID

Backfill to be free placed in layers not deeper than 300mm and well compacted

Min 300mm

Min 150mm

Selected fill of granular material free from stones larger than 40mm

Min 100mm

Granular material to be taken up to half depth of pipe

Bed pipe on min 100mm deep granular material

Min 100mm

min 100mm granular

If your drainage is close to your foundations then you will be required to place additional concrete as indicated on the following sections.

FOUNDATIONS NEAR DRAINS

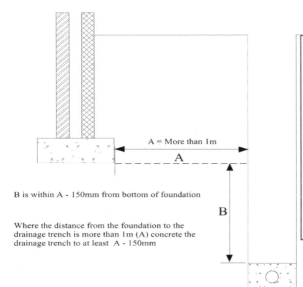

A = More than 1m

A

B is within A - 150mm from bottom of foundation

B

Where the distance from the foundation to the
drainage trench is more than 1m (A) concrete the
drainage trench to at least A - 150mm

Once all your drainage is installed and prior to occupation you will be required to have your underground drainage tested, to ensure there are no leaks.

The most common and easiest way to achieve this is by way of a water test.

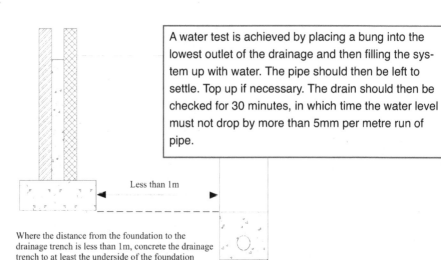

Less than 1m

A water test is achieved by placing a bung into the lowest outlet of the drainage and then filling the system up with water. The pipe should then be left to settle. Top up if necessary. The drain should then be checked for 30 minutes, in which time the water level must not drop by more than 5mm per metre run of pipe.

Where the distance from the foundation to the
drainage trench is less than 1m, concrete the drainage
trench to at least the underside of the foundation

Substructure is the brick and block work which is built from the foundations up to the DPC (Damp Proof Course). There are many considerations to be taken into account while constructing your substructure walls in preparation for a floor slab:

- Position of internal drainage
- Incoming services
- Contaminated ground
- DPC and DPM at correct level
- Correct Mortar used
- Correct blocks and bricks used
- Type of floor slab construction
- Correct Insulation is used
- Allowing for underfloor heating

Raft Foundation

If your chosen method of construction is a Raft foundation, most of your substructure and floor slab will all be cast as one unit. However the points listed still need to be taken into consideration

Position of Internal Drainage

Consult your drainage layout drawings making sure that any internal drainage is correctly laid, and that all drainage that passes through internal and external walls has correct lintels built in over the top.

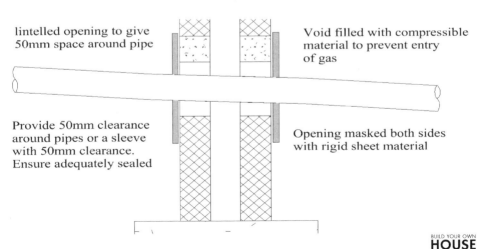

PIPES PASSING THROUGH
WALL (LINTEL)

lintelled opening to give
50mm space around pipe

Void filled with compressible
material to prevent entry
of gas

Provide 50mm clearance
around pipes or a sleeve
with 50mm clearance.
Ensure adequately sealed

Opening masked both sides
with rigid sheet material

BUILD YOUR OWN
HOUSE

Have your internal drainage tested and inspected before you concrete your Floor Slab. This is important as once a slab is cast or installed it can be costly to have to carry out any remedial work.

Incoming Services - This will probably only involve your incoming water supply, as gas, electric and media usually enters newly-built properties above DPC (damp proof course). The exception would be apartments where incoming services are normally located in a riser or a specially constructed plant room. Incoming water has to have its own duct and when installed it needs to be properly insulated.

Contaminated Ground - If the ground is found to be contaminated then precautions should be taken. Any action taken must be approved by Local Building Control and your Warranty provider. There are certain parts of the country where Radon Gas has been identified.

Radon is a colourless odourless radioactive gas. It occurs naturally and is thought to be a risk to health. If a high level of Radon has been identified then precautions need to be taken. Public Health England has prepared maps indicating the chance of a building having a high Radon level. These maps cover England, Wales, Scotland and Northern Ireland and can be viewed at:

www.UKradon.org

The **BRE** (Building Research Establishment) has produced a range of cost-effective and practical solutions to prevent radon entry into new and existing homes. These processes can be purchased from their website. There are many systems on the market should gas prevention be required.

DPC and DPM at correct level - The Damp Proof Course should be inserted a minimum of 150mm above the finished ground level around your finished property. Depending on the nature of any slopes on a site this may increase quite dramatically; sometimes extra face brickwork may be required.

You must ensure that your Damp Proof Membrane (DPM) correctly laps with the DPC. If polyethylene sheet is to be used as your damp proof membrane then it must not be less than 1200 gauge (0.3mm)

Correct Mortar - Mortar for the use below DPC is a different mix from mortars that are used above DPC. If you are in any doubt of a suitable mix you should follow recommendations given in BS EN 1996-1-1.

Mortar used below DPC would usually be class 6. General purpose mortar is class 1. Where the ground, ground water or the masonry that is to be used contains levels of sulphates, the mortar should be made with sulphate resisting cement.

Correct bricks and blocks used - Walls below DPC should be of a design to allow them to support their intended load and should be resistant to any sulphates that may be present. The walls should also be resistant to frost.

All bricks and blocks should have a compressive strength not less than 7.3N/mm2. On taller buildings the compressive strength of the bricks and blocks may need to be increased.

The compressive strengths of your bricks and blocks are normally indicated on your building regulation drawings.

Walls that are constructed below ground and will be permanently covered over can be constructed with trench blocks. Trench blocks are the total width of the wall construction, which save time on having to construct an inner and an outer leaf of brick and block work. Trench blocks can only be used to a depth below 225mm from DPC, as a clear cavity at 225mm below DPC needs to be maintained.

Type of floor construction - Ground bearing floor slab may only be used if the trenches are backfilled with properly compacted material, the infill is less than 600mm in depth and properly compacted and suitable to support a floor slab and any additional loads.

SOLID GROUND FLOOR

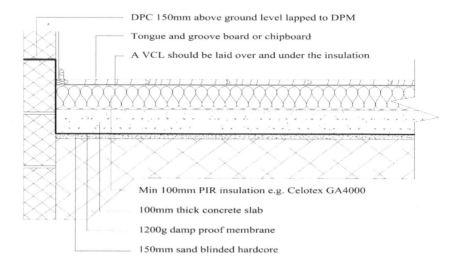

DPC 150mm above ground level lapped to DPM

Tongue and groove board or chipboard

A VCL should be laid over and under the insulation

Min 100mm PIR insulation e.g. Celotex GA4000

100mm thick concrete slab

1200g damp proof membrane

150mm sand blinded hardcore

BEAM AND BLOCK FLOOR

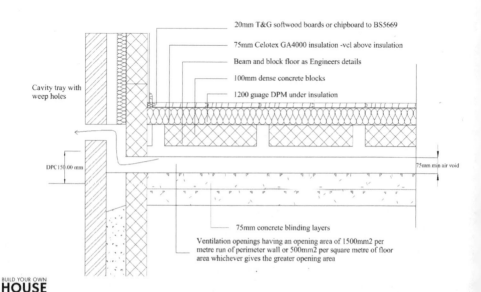

20mm T&G softwood boards or chipboard to BS5669

75mm Celotex GA4000 insulation -vcl above insulation

Beam and block floor as Engineers details

100mm dense concrete blocks

1200 guage DPM under insulation

Cavity tray with weep holes

DPC150.00 mm

75mm min air void

75mm concrete blinding layers

Ventilation openings having an opening area of 1500mm2 per metre run of perimeter wall or 500mm2 per square metre of floor area whichever gives the greater opening area

If more than 600mm of fill is required then the floor will need to be of a suspended construction. If the floor is suspended it will be supported by the internal cavity wall. If a floor slab is to be a concrete slab then reinforcing mesh will need to be introduced.

Another suspended Floor Slab could consist of engineered concrete beams and solid block construction. If this method is to be adopted you must allow for an adequate void to allow air flow and by introducing air bricks to the perimeter of your dwelling.

TIMBER SUSPENDED FLOOR

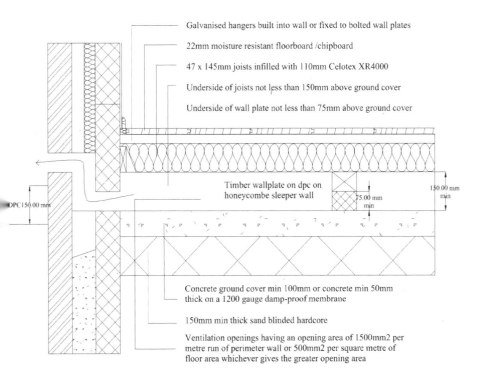

Galvanised hangers built into wall or fixed to bolted wall plates

22mm moisture resistant floorboard /chipboard

47 x 145mm joists infilled with 110mm Celotex XR4000

Underside of joists not less than 150mm above ground cover

Underside of wall plate not less than 75mm above ground cover

Timber wallplate on dpc on honeycombe sleeper wall

75.00 mm min

150.00 mm min

DPC 150.00 mm

Concrete ground cover min 100mm or concrete min 50mm thick on a 1200 gauge damp-proof membrane

150mm min thick sand blinded hardcore

Ventilation openings having an opening area of 1500mm2 per metre run of perimeter wall or 500mm2 per square metre of floor area whichever gives the greater opening area

If your dwelling is to have an integral garage then your garage floor slab will need to be lower than the finished floor slab of the main dwelling. 150mm is usual and should slope towards the front of the garage.

BUILD YOUR OWN
HOUSE

SOLID GARAGE FLOOR

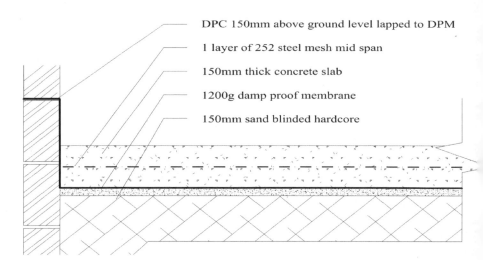

DPC 150mm above ground level lapped to DPM

1 layer of 252 steel mesh mid span

150mm thick concrete slab

1200g damp proof membrane

150mm sand blinded hardcore

Correct Insulation- Depending on the sustainable code you are building to, this will influence the type and thickness of the insulation required under your floor slab. There are many different products now on the market that will allow you to achieve your required thermal conductivity design value. The insulation can be placed either under or on top of your concrete floor, depending on the type of floor construction method you are using.

Allow for under floor heating- If you are intending to have under floor heating, your concrete floor slab will be lower in relation to the DPC to allow for insulation, heating loops and floor screed. When you come to screed your floor after the heating pipes have been laid, you will have a choice of a semi dry screed mix, which is hand laid, or a flow screed.

Sand and cement screeds are normally laid to depth of 75mm and are laid by hand. By contrast flow screeds, which are sometimes known as liquid or self-levelling screeds, can be laid to a depth of only 40mm. However this may not be sufficient to adequately cover the heating loops.

Superstructure and Scaffold

The definition of the word Superstructure in relation to this book is all external and internal load-bearing walls including: floors, cavity insulation, window openings plus any structural elements - lintels, ties and any structural steel work that may be required.

Construction of external and internal walls always goes hand-in-hand with scaffold erection. Before you start building any external walls you must also prepare a suitable base for a scaffold to be erected upon.

Once your Floor Slab is complete and all your drainage has been connected, you will then need to backfill and level the ground around your plot. Place and compact a suitable amount of stone to give you a firm base. You will need to stone and compact an area about 2 metres wide around the full perimeter of your plot. Try to place the stone at a level that would be ready to lay any paving on. By doing this it will save you having to carry out the same operation of levelling and compacting stone when you are ready to introduce paths and walkways, later on in your project.

The type of scaffold you will require will depend on the type of external wall construction you will be using. You will need to give details of your intended construction method to your scaffold contractor so he can accommodate your requirements.

The main types of external wall construction:

- Brick and Block
- Block and Render
- Natural walling stone
- Coursed Stone
- Timber Frame
- SIPS (Structural Insulated Panels)
- ICF (Insulated Concrete Formwork)

BUILD YOUR OWN
HOUSE

All these types of wall construction will be required to meet a 'U-value', being the minimum heat loss values. U-values are a measure of heat loss in a building. The higher the U-value the worse the performance of the building envelope. A low U-value would indicate higher levels of insulation. External walls form a large area of the envelope of a dwelling so it is important to achieve a low U-value. Building regulations determine the maximum allowed U-value.

Brick and Block
Brick and Block external wall construction is the most common construction method for a new built dwelling, and it is generally considered to be the most cost-effective build. Insulation can be either partial or full fill cavity.

Here are standard details:

PARTIAL FILL CAVITY WALL

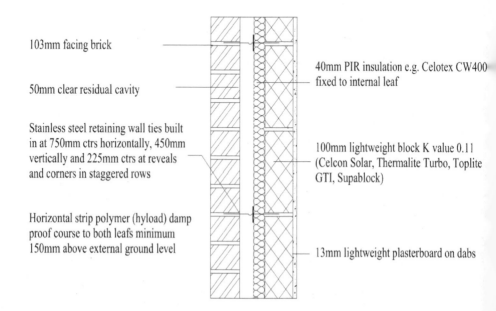

103mm facing brick

50mm clear residual cavity

Stainless steel retaining wall ties built in at 750mm ctrs horizontally, 450mm vertically and 225mm ctrs at reveals and corners in staggered rows

Horizontal strip polymer (hyload) damp proof course to both leafs minimum 150mm above external ground level

40mm PIR insulation e.g. Celotex CW400 fixed to internal leaf

100mm lightweight block K value 0.11 (Celcon Solar, Thermalite Turbo, Toplite GTI, Supablock)

13mm lightweight plasterboard on dabs

BUILD YOUR OWN
HOUSE

FULL FILL CAVITY WALL

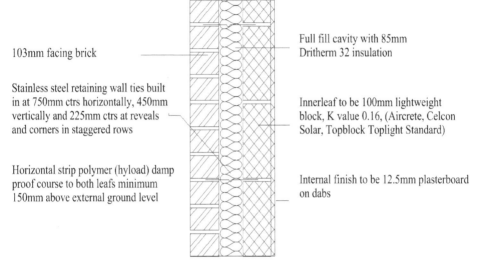

103mm facing brick

Stainless steel retaining wall ties built in at 750mm ctrs horizontally, 450mm vertically and 225mm ctrs at reveals and corners in staggered rows

Horizontal strip polymer (hyload) damp proof course to both leafs minimum 150mm above external ground level

Full fill cavity with 85mm Dritherm 32 insulation

Innerleaf to be 100mm lightweight block, K value 0.16, (Aircrete, Celcon Solar, Topblock Toplight Standard)

Internal finish to be 12.5mm plasterboard on dabs

With todays emphasis being on insulation and to minimise heat loss it is not uncommon to see additional insulation introduced internally on to the block work.

Block and Render

If using Block and Render, two skins of block work should be built, including the required amount of cavity insulation. Sometimes with Block and Render the insulation is fixed to the outside of the block work and render is applied directly onto the insulation. A bell cast bead needs to be fixed above all window and door openings and along the DPC. Render below DPC will need to be of a suitable mix, to withstand frost and surface water.

Scaffolding will have to be designed and adapted if necessary, to allow the rendering to be applied.There are many different types of render finishes and colours available, but note that you will probably require approval of render finish from your planning department.

BUILD YOUR OWN
HOUSE

Natural Walling Stone

If you intend to face your new dwelling with natural walling stone, you will have to widen your foundations accordingly. The usual construction method would be 2 skins of block work with a cavity, incorporating all necessary insulation and faced with 200mm of random natural stone. Stone window, door heads and cills will be required. The roof construction must also take into consideration the stone facing.

Coursed Stone

Coursed stone unlike natural stone can be purchased and delivered to site ready to be laid. Normally being 100mm wide and being of such sizes to allow them to be laid forming the outer leaf of cavity construction.

There are many variations of size and colour of stone face on the market; suitable approval will be required from your local planning department.

Stone Face
If you intend to have your dwelling stone faced, it needs to be incorporated at the design stage

Timber Frame

Timber Frame construction generally comes in a kit form and is erected in panels. Timber frame construction is a far quicker process of erecting a dwelling and getting it to a water-tight stage, although it is thought to be more expensive than traditional masonry construction.

Timber framed houses will be structurally designed and the design will be sub-

Timber frame kits are usually on a supply and erect basis and the supplier will require the scaffolding to be fully erected before the kit arrives on site. Once the kit arrives on site the panels will be craned into position. It is usual for the roof to be supplied and constructed as part of the timber framed kit. All the upper floors including flooring is usually incorporated as part of the timber framed kit.

Once the timber kit has been erected it can be clad in a variety of finishes. Below are some examples showing the construction method:

RENDERED TIMBER FRAMED WALL

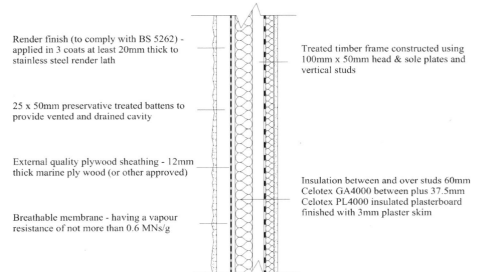

Render finish (to comply with BS 5262) - applied in 3 coats at least 20mm thick to stainless steel render lath

Treated timber frame constructed using 100mm x 50mm head & sole plates and vertical studs

25 x 50mm preservative treated battens to provide vented and drained cavity

External quality plywood sheathing - 12mm thick marine ply wood (or other approved)

Insulation between and over studs 60mm Celotex GA4000 between plus 37.5mm Celotex PL4000 insulated plasterboard finished with 3mm plaster skim

Breathable membrane - having a vapour resistance of not more than 0.6 MNs/g

BRICK FINISH TIMBER FRAMED WALL

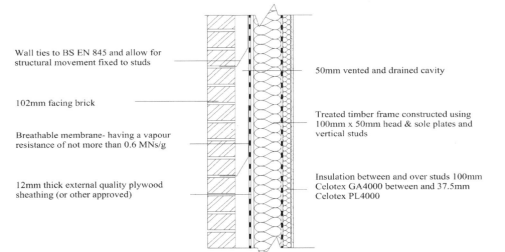

Wall ties to BS EN 845 and allow for structural movement fixed to studs

50mm vented and drained cavity

102mm facing brick

Treated timber frame constructed using 100mm x 50mm head & sole plates and vertical studs

Breathable membrane- having a vapour resistance of not more than 0.6 MNs/g

12mm thick external quality plywood sheathing (or other approved)

Insulation between and over studs 100mm Celotex GA4000 between and 37.5mm Celotex PL4000

SIPS (Structural Insulated Panels): SIPS are prefabricated, high performance, lightweight panels that can be used in floors, walls and roofs for residential buildings; they are also used for commercial buildings.The panels are made up from two high density facings, typically Orientated Strand Board (OSB) which is bonded on both sides of a low density, cellular core.The panels are constructed in such a way to give a full structural design.The onsite construction process is very similar to timber frame construction, where a fully erected scaffold will be required prior to erection and the panels will be craned into position.The panels can then be clad in a variety of materials or rendered.

ICF (Insulated Concrete Formwork): ICF is based on hollow lightweight block components that lock together without the need for a mortar bed. It provides a system into which concrete can be poured. The block is formed of sheets of insulation materials, normally expanded polystyrene tied together with plastic or steel ties or an integral web of the same insulation. Once the concrete has been poured the thermal insulation remains in place providing U-values down to as low as 0.11 w/m2k, which is ideal for helping to achieve level 6 in the code for sustainable homes.

The system is also an approved walling system for basements.

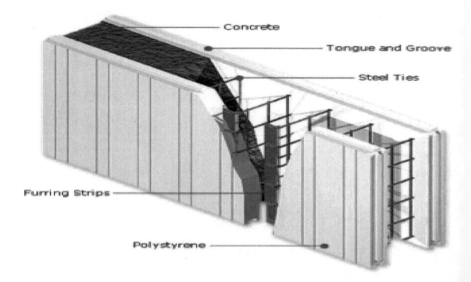

Lintels

All lintels need to be structurally designed for their intended use; most good builders merchants will be able to recommend the correct lintel for the intended use. When placing lintels make sure they achieve the minimum bearing which is usually 150mm at each end. Make sure lintels are suitably insulated to prevent any cold bridging. Make sure cavity trays, stop ends and weep vents are correctly installed. Below is a typical detailed section of a lintel above a window.

WINDOW HEAD AND LINTEL

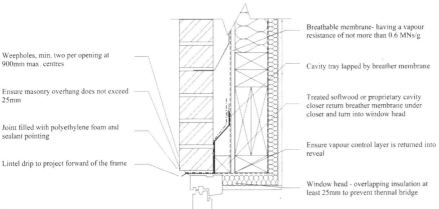

Weepholes, min. two per opening at 900mm max. centres

Ensure masonry overhang does not exceed 25mm

Joint filled with polyethylene foam and sealant pointing

Lintel drip to project forward of the frame

Breathable membrane- having a vapour resistance of not more than 0.6 MNs/g

Cavity tray lapped by breather membrane

Treated softwood or proprietary cavity closer return breather membrane under closer and turn into window head

Ensure vapour control layer is returned into reveal

Window head - overlapping insulation at least 25mm to prevent thermal bridge

Steelwork

Sometimes it may be necessary to introduce steelwork into a new dwelling. Steel work will be designed specifically for the job intended, and will be required to be fabricated off site. Pad stones will have to be introduced for any steelwork to sit on; pad stones are normally a solid high density concrete block. Alternatively a minimum of 3 courses of engineering brick can be used.

Floor Joists

You will generally have the option of engineered floors or traditional timber. Engineered joists are becoming ever popular. They have the advantage of being lighter, no shrinkage, longer spans can be achieved and you can fix your flooring at the same time that you install your joists as services can pass through the middle of them.

BUILD YOUR OWN
HOUSE

Superstructure and Scaffold

Traditional floor joists should be adequate for the spans and imposed loads. All structural timber for solid floor joists are specified as Class 16 or Class 24. Maximum permitted spans for joists, giving the size required, can be found in the TRADA technologies publication "span tables for solid timber members in floors, ceilings and roofs (excluding trussed rafter roofs) for dwellings".

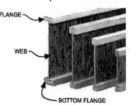

Maximum clear span of floor joists (m): Timber strength class C16									**C16**
	Dead Load [kN/m²] excluding the self weight of the joist								
	Not more than 0.25			More than 0.25 but not more than 0.50			More than 0.50 but not more than 1.25		
Size of joist (mm x mm)	Spacing of joists (mm)								
	400	450	600	400	450	600	400	450	600
38 x 97	1.83	1.69	1.30	1.72	1.56	1.21	1.42	1.30	1.04
38 x 120	2.48	2.39	1.93	2.37	2.22	1.76	1.95	1.79	1.45
38 x 145	2.98	2.87	2.51	2.85	2.71	2.33	2.45	2.29	1.87
38 x 170	3.44	3.31	2.87	3.28	3.10	2.69	2.81	2.65	2.27
38 x 195	3.94	3.75	3.26		3.52	3.06	3.19	3.01	2.61
38 x 220	4.43	4.19	3.65	4.16	3.93	3.42	3.57	3.37	2.92
47 x 97	2.02	1.91	1.58	1.92	1.82	1.46	1.67	1.53	1.23
47 x 120	2.66	2.56	2.30	2.55	2.45	2.09	2.26	2.08	1.70
47 x 145	3.20	3.08	2.79	3.06	2.95	2.61	2.72	2.57	2.17
47 x 170	3.69	3.55	3.19	3.53	3.40	2.99	3.12	2.94	2.55
47 x 195	4.22	4.06	3.62	4.04	3.89	3.39	3.54	3.34	2.90
47 x 220	4.72	4.57	4.04	4.55	4.35	3.79	3.95	3.74	3.24
50 x 97	2.08	1.97	1.67	1.98	1.87	1.54	1.74	1.60	1.29
50 x 120	2.72	2.62	2.37	2.60	2.50	2.19	2.33	2.17	1.77
50 x 145	3.27	3.14	2.86	3.13	3.01	2.69	2.81	2.65	2.27
50 x 170	3.77	3.62	3.29	3.61	3.47	3.08	3.21	3.03	2.63
50 x 195	4.31	4.15	3.73	4.13	3.97	3.50	3.65	3.44	2.99
50 x 220	4.79	4.66	4.17	4.64	4.47	3.91	4.07	3.85	3.35
63 x 97	2.32	2.20	1.92	2.19	2.08	1.82	1.93	1.84	1.53
63 x 120	2.93	2.82	2.57	2.81	2.70	2.45	2.53	2.43	2.09
63 x 145	3.52	3.39	3.08	3.37	3.24	2.95	3.04	2.92	2.58
63 x 170	4.06	3.91	3.56	3.89	3.74	3.40	3.50	3.37	2.95
63 x 195	4.63	4.47	4.07	4.44	4.28	3.90	4.01	3.85	3.35
63 x 220	5.06	4.92	4.58	4.91	4.77	4.37	4.51	4.30	3.75
75 x 120	3.10	2.99	2.72	2.97	2.86	2.60	2.68	2.58	2.33
75 x 145	3.72	3.58	3.27	3.56	3.43	3.13	3.22	3.09	2.81
75 x 170	4.28	4.13	3.77	4.11	3.96	3.61	3.71	3.57	3.21
75 x 195	4.83	4.70	4.31	4.68	4.52	4.13	4.24	4.08	3.65
75 x 220	5.27	5.13	4.79	5.11	4.97	4.64	4.74	4.60	4.07
CLS/ALS									
38 x 140	2.84	2.73	2.40	2.72	2.59	2.17	2.33	2.15	1.75
38 x 184	3.72	3.56	3.09	3.53	3.33	2.90	3.02	2.85	2.47
38 x 235	4.71	4.46	3.89	4.43	4.18	3.64	3.80	3.59	3.11

Superstructure and Scaffold

Maximum clear span of floor joists (m): Timber strength class C24

C24

Size of joist (mm x mm)	Dead Load [kN/m²] excluding the self weight of the joist								
	Not more than 0.25			More than 0.25 but not more than 0.50			More than 0.50 but not more than 1.25		
	Spacing of joists (mm)								
	400	450	600	400	450	600	400	450	600
38 x 97	1.94	1.83	1.59	1.84	1.74	1.51	1.64	1.55	1.36
38 x 120	2.58	2.48	2.20	2.47	2.37	2.08	2.18	2.07	1.83
38 x 145	3.10	2.98	2.71	2.97	2.85	2.59	2.67	2.56	2.31
38 x 170	3.58	3.44	3.13	3.43	3.29	2.99	3.08	2.96	2.68
38 x 195	4.10	3.94	3.58	3.92	3.77	3.42	3.53	3.39	3.07
38 x 220	4.61	4.44	4.03	4.41	4.25	3.86	3.97	3.82	3.46
47 x 97	2.14	2.03	1.76	2.03	1.92	1.68	1.80	1.71	1.50
47 x 120	2.77	2.66	2.42	2.65	2.55	2.29	2.38	2.27	2.01
47 x 145	3.33	3.20	2.91	3.19	3.06	2.78	2.87	2.75	2.50
47 x 170	3.84	3.69	3.36	3.67	3.54	3.21	3.31	3.18	2.88
47 x 195	4.39	4.22	3.85	4.20	4.05	3.68	3.79	3.64	3.30
47 x 220	4.86	4.73	4.33	4.71	4.55	4.14	4.26	4.10	3.72
50 x 97	2.20	2.09	1.82	2.08	1.98	1.73	1.84	1.75	1.54
50 x 120	2.83	2.72	2.47	2.71	2.60	2.36	2.43	2.33	2.06
50 x 145	3.39	3.27	2.97	3.25	3.13	2.84	2.93	2.81	2.55
50 x 170	3.91	3.77	3.43	3.75	3.61	3.28	3.38	3.25	2.94
50 x 195	4.47	4.31	3.92	4.29	4.13	3.75	3.86	3.72	3.37
50 x 220	4.93	4.80	4.42	4.78	4.64	4.23	4.35	4.18	3.80
63 x 97	2.43	2.32	2.03	2.31	2.19	1.93	2.03	1.93	1.71
63 x 120	3.05	2.93	2.67	2.92	2.81	2.55	2.63	2.53	2.27
63 x 145	3.67	3.52	3.21	3.50	3.37	3.07	3.16	3.04	2.76
63 x 170	4.21	4.06	3.70	4.04	3.89	3.54	3.64	3.51	3.19
63 x 195	4.77	4.64	4.23	4.61	4.45	4.05	4.17	4.01	3.65
63 x 220	5.20	5.06	4.73	5.05	4.91	4.56	4.68	4.51	4.11
75 x 120	3.22	3.10	2.83	3.09	2.97	2.71	2.78	2.68	2.43
75 x 145	3.86	3.72	3.39	3.70	3.57	3.25	3.34	3.22	2.93
75 x 170	4.45	4.29	3.91	4.27	4.11	3.75	3.86	3.71	3.38
75 x 195	4.97	4.83	4.47	4.82	4.69	4.29	4.41	4.25	3.86
75 x 220	5.42	5.27	4.93	5.25	5.11	4.78	4.88	4.74	4.35
CLS/ALS									
38 x 140	2.96	2.84	2.58	2.83	2.72	2.47	2.54	2.44	2.17
38 x 184	3.87	3.72	3.38	3.70	3.56	3.23	3.33	3.20	2.90
38 x 235	4.85	4.71	4.31	4.70	4.54	4.12	4.24	4.08	3.70

Solid floor joists should not be spaced at centres exceeding 600mm and with solid floor joists you will not be able to lay the floors until you have installed your pipe work. Regardless of which joist system you are using you will still need to fix or build in all joist hangers that may be required, plus making sure all noggins are in place. This will all have to be inspected before they are covered in. If your floor joists are at 600mm centres then you will need to use 22mm flooring.

Window and Door Openings

Windows are generally all fitted at the same time, which is normally after the roof is on. When building window and door openings make sure the opening is slightly larger than the window itself; most bricklayers allow an extra 10mm.

Before you insert your windows you will need insulated cavity closers fitted. You can get insulated formers that you build in during construction.

Wall Ties

Walls Ties should be long enough to be embedded at least 500mm into each leaf. All wall ties should be stainless steel or non-ferrous and should be in accordance with **BS EN 12588.** Ties should be spaced a maximum of 900mm apart horizontally and 450mm vertically. At all openings and movement joints wall ties should be spaced a maximum of 300mm vertically.

Scaffolding

Scaffolding should always be undertaken by a qualified contractor and once erected it may not be removed or adapted by anyone apart from the scaffold contractor.

Working At Height regulations are a hot topic, and have been for some time. Even self-build projects will get visits from the HSE (Health and Safety Executive) and working at heights is an area that will get looked at, as it is considered high risk.

When you are in discussions with a scaffold contractor make them aware of your requirements. The contractor will need to be informed of the method of construction to enable them to price for a suitable scaffold. They will also need to know the duration that the scaffolding is required. Always try to allow some time for delays when negotiating a hire period.

Scaffolding needs to be erected to prevent any falls from height. Hand rails, toe boards and brick guards will be fitted accordingly and must not be removed while the scaffold is in use.

Discuss with the scaffolding contractor what areas of the scaffold you will need to load materials; they will then accommodate you with suitable loading bays. It is also a good idea to have scaffold designed so you can gain access to the inside of the property.

When building traditionally your scaffold will be erected in lifts as your dwelling progresses. It will probably require adapting to accommodate the roof installation and any external cladding or render.

If you are building timber frame or using SIPS then you will probably have to get your scaffold fully erected before the kits arrive on site.

There are various types of scaffolding available for hire, the most common being tube and fitting. Some scaffold contractors prefer system scaffolds; this is where the components lock together without the need for further fittings. Your scaffolding contractor will be able to advise on the best scaffold that is suited for your project.

Every time your scaffold contractor attends site to erect scaffold or make an adaption make sure he gives you a hand over certificate before he leaves. This will ensure your scaffold is fit for purpose.

Sometimes scaffolders will have a tag on the scaffolding indicating if the scaffold is fit for use or not, this is known as a scaff tag.

Your scaffold contractor should ensure your scaffold is inspected on a weekly basis.

Scaffolds
All scaffolding should comply with Working At Height regulations 2005

Listed below are the issues which have to be considered when designing a roof:

- Type of roof construction
- Room in a roof
- Roof pitch
- Dormer Windows
- Roof lights
- Soffits and Fascias
- Ventilation
- Roof coverings

Type of roof construction
This can be split into four main types:

1 – Trussed Roofs. **2** – Traditional Hand Cut Roofs.
3 – Panelised Roofing System. **4** – Lower Roofs.

Trussed Roofs – These are a quick and cost-effective way of installing a roof and nowadays are the preferred choice for most builders. Below is a typical section of a roof truss, along with general notes:

FINK TRUSS ROOF

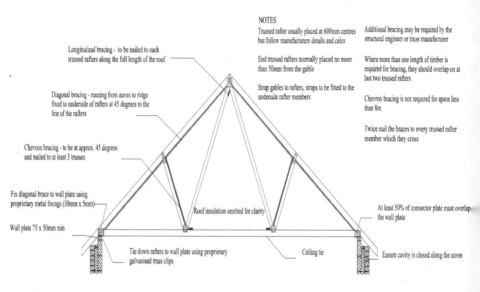

NOTES

Trussed rafter usually placed at 600mm centres but follow manufacturers details and calcs

Additional bracing may be required by the structural engineer or truss manufacturer

End trussed rafters normally placed no more than 50mm from the gable

Where more than one length of timber is required for bracing, they should overlap on at last two trussed rafters

Strap gables to rafters, straps to be fitted to the underside rafter members

Chevron bracing is not required for spans less than 8m

Twice nail the braces to every trussed rafter member which they cross

Longitudinal bracing - to be nailed to each trussed rafters along the full length of the roof

Diagonal bracing - running from eaves to ridge fixed to underside of rafters at 45 degrees to the line of the rafters

Chevron bracing - to be at approx. 45 degrees and nailed to at least 3 trusses

Fix diagonal brace to wall plate using proprietary metal fixings (30mm x 5mm)

Wall plate 75 x 50mm min

Roof insulation omitted for clarity

At least 50% of connector plate must overlap the wall plate

Tie down rafters to wall plate using proprietary galvanised truss clips

Ceiling tie

Ensure cavity is closed along the eaves

Trusses are designed and made by specialist manufacturers. To ensure they are designed and fabricated correctly for their intended use, certain design information will be required:

● Required roof pitch
● Roof span
● Height and location of the roof, with references to any unusual wind conditions
● Intended roof covering
● The method and position of supporting the trusses
● Your required Eaves Detail (Below is a typical Eaves Detail)

EAVES DETAIL

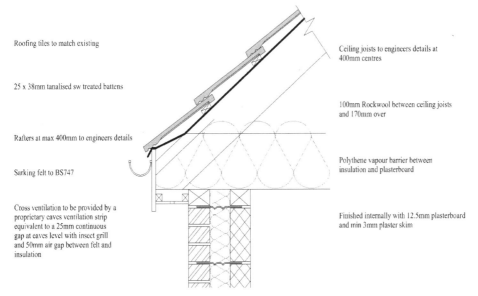

Roofing tiles to match existing

25 x 38mm tanalised sw treated battens

Rafters at max 400mm to engineers details

Sarking felt to BS747

Cross ventilation to be provided by a proprietary eaves ventilation strip equivalent to a 25mm continuous gap at eaves level with insect grill and 50mm air gap between felt and insulation

Ceiling joists to engineers details at 400mm centres

100mm Rockwool between ceiling joists and 170mm over

Polythene vapour barrier between insulation and plasterboard

Finished internally with 12.5mm plasterboard and min 3mm plaster skim

● Position of any chimneys or flues
● Size and position of any water tanks or other equipment that may be installed in the loft area
● Dormer positions and sizes
● Position and sizes of roof lights
● Are attic trusses required?
● Type of timber treatment

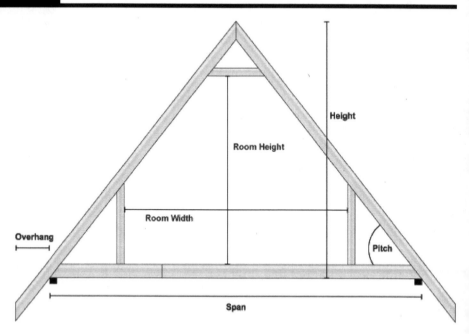

Truss manufacturers are used to dealing with all the above issues and will be able to design and advise accordingly. Once you have received your design you will need to get it approved by local building control and your warranty provider. Because of the size and weight of some roof trusses it is advisable to crane them into position; each truss will have its weight indicated on it, which will aid you in deciding whether a crane would be required.

You must install your roof to the manufacturer's design, ensuring all bracing is placed and fixed in the correct positions. The spacing of roof trusses should not exceed 600mm. If multiple trusses are indicated fixed together, they should be either fixed during the manufacturing process or if they are to be fixed on site, fully detailed fixing arrangements should be supplied by the manufacturer.

Roof Truss
You must have your wall plates bedded on and straps fitted before you start installing roof trusses

Traditional Hand Cut Roofs – Hand cut roofs are made up from loose timbers, cut and fitted on site. The size and position of the roof members will still be carried out to an approved design. Like trussed roofs you are still required to have your design approved by local building control and your warranty provider. Inserted is a typical plan of a Hand Cut Roof, showing all the components:

CUT PURLIN ROOF (PLAN)

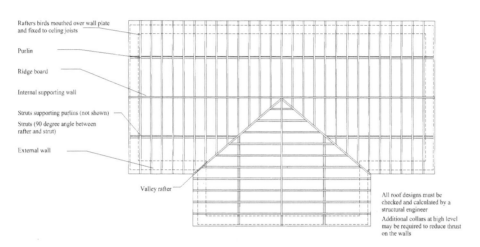

Rafters birds mouthed over wall plate and fixed to celing joists

Purlin

Ridge board

Internal supporting wall

Struts supporting purlins (not shown)

Struts (90 degree angle between rafter and strut)

External wall

Valley rafter

All roof designs must be checked and calculated by a structural engineer

Additional collars at high level may be required to reduce thrust on the walls

All roof timbers need to be adequately treated and to be of the correct grade. Before constructing your roof all wall plates should be bedded down and fixing straps positioned correctly. Hand cut roofs are more labour-intensive than trussed roofs; however you will rarely need the use of a crane unless steelwork needs to be introduced to the structure.

Panelised Roofing System – The panels are factory made incorporating necessary insulation; as part of the system the gable walls, known as spandrel panels, are also included. Manufacturers will be able to accommodate any dormers or roof lights that you may require. Panelised Roof Systems usually come as a supply and fix package, including organising craneage. The system can leave you with an insulated water-tight roof in a day, not including roof covering i.e. slate or tiles. You will need to have wall plates bedded on to the whole of the perimeter, including gable ends, and fixed down with wall plate straps prior to installation of the panels. You will also need all scaffolding in place, including table lifts on the gable ends prior to roof installation.

The insulated panels provide an extremely high thermal performance and U – values can be as low as 0.10W/m2K. There is minimal thermal bridging compared to conventional construction and the insulation will not sag over time.

Lower Roofs – Lower Roofs are normally constructed once the main structure of a dwelling has been built and the main scaffolding removed. Lower Roofs cover all the single storey parts of a dwelling; they still need to be structurally designed and approved by local building control and your warranty provider. They will need to be insulated to prevent heat loss. Lower Roofs are not always of the same design or pitch as the main roof. You must ensure that while you are building the main structure you build in cavity trays at the correct heights and positions to allow lower roofs to abut the walls correctly.

Below are typical sections of lower roofs with notes:

FLAT ROOF / WALL ABUTMENT

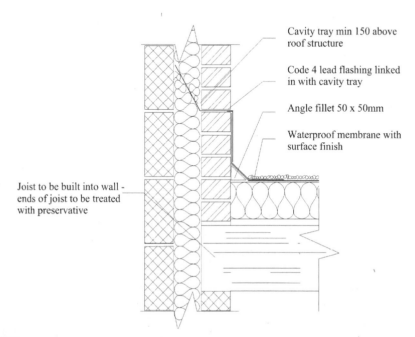

Cavity tray min 150 above roof structure

Code 4 lead flashing linked in with cavity tray

Angle fillet 50 x 50mm

Waterproof membrane with surface finish

Joist to be built into wall - ends of joist to be treated with preservative

MONO-PITCHED ROOF

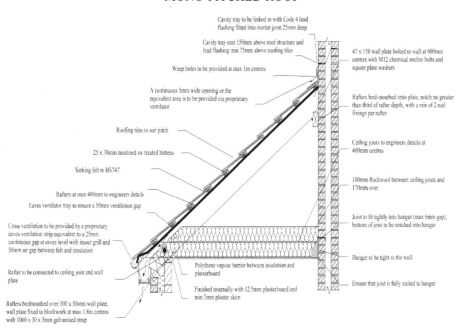

Cavity tray to be linked in with Code 4 lead flashing fitted into mortar joint 25mm deep

Cavity tray min 150mm above roof structure and lead flashing min 75mm above roofing tiles

Weep holes to be provided at max 1m centres

A continuous 5mm wide opening or the equivalent area is to be provided via proprietary ventilator

Roofing tiles to suit pitch

25 x 38mm tanalised sw treated battens

Sarking felt to BS747

Rafters at max 400mm to engineers details

Eaves ventilator tray to ensure a 50mm ventilation gap

Cross ventilation to be provided by a proprietary eaves ventilation strip equivalent to a 25mm continuous gap at eaves level with insect grill and 50mm air gap between felt and insulation

Rafter to be connected to ceiling joist and wall plate

Rafters birdmouthed over 100 x 50mm wall plate, wall plate fixed to blockwork at max 1.8m centres with 1000 x 30 x 5mm galvanised strap

47 x 150 wall plate bolted to wall at 600mm centres with M12 chemical anchor bolts and square plate washers

Rafters bird-mouthed onto plate, notch no greater than third of rafter depth, with a min of 2 nail fixings per rafter

Ceiling joists to engineers details at 400mm centres

100mm Rockwool between ceiling joists and 170mm over

Joist to fit tightly into hanger (max 6mm gap), bottom of joist to be notched into hanger

Hanger to be tight to the wall

Ensure that joist is fully nailed to hanger

Polythene vapour barrier between insulation and plasterboard

Finished internally with 12.5mm plasterboard and min 3mm plaster skin

If your main roof is going to be used as a habitable room then it will need to be insulated between the rafters, unlike non habitable loft spaces which only require insulating across the ceiling joists.If you are intending to use your roof space for additional rooms you may introduce dormers and roof lights into your roof. Any dormers you introduce into your roof will require planning permission but generally roof lights do not.

ROOF COVERINGS
There are many choices of roof coverings the most common being..

●Slates ●Clay Tiles ●Concrete Tiles ●Thatch

Whatever your choice of roof covering it will need approval from your planning department. Planners will usually look at the type of material that is being used locally to allow your new dwelling to blend with surrounding properties, particularly if you are in a conservation area.

SLATE ROOFS

Slate is generally thought to be a very high quality roof covering and this is reflected in the price, especially if you are planning on using local slate. There are cheaper alternatives on the market, generally imported from places such as Spain or Brazil. Apart from the cost of buying slate the fixing is a costly process, as it usually has to be sorted, sized and holed.

Slate does have advantages over other roof coverings. Apart from its appearance it has a long lifespan; a good slate roof can be expected to have a lifespan of 150 years or more.

Slate is also fire-resistant; slate is also waterproof.

Depending on the head lap and its size, slate can be laid to a minimum pitch of 20 degrees.

When fixing slate you should always use aluminium or copper nails, with a minimum batten size of 25x50mm. Slate can be blue or green so make sure you purchase the correct colour to give yourself the desired effect.

The diagram below indicates head lap:

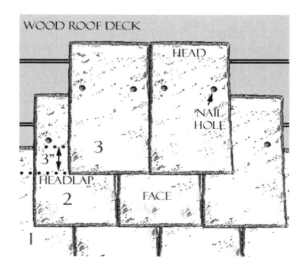

Even on a newly-built house it is not uncommon to purchase second hand slate. It is usually sold by the ton; expect to get something like 16 metres square per ton.

If you are going to fix the slate yourself always carry out the work ensuring you have the recommended head lap for your roof pitch.

CLAY ROOF TILES

Clay Tiled roofs are another natural product pleasing to the eye. It always has the appearance of a premier product.

Clay is a natural material, which in the form of clay tiles has played an integral role in the UK's built environment for over 700 years. Clay tiles are a durable and sustainable product that improves with age and weathering. There are many different colours of clay tiles and many of the colours are unique to their locality. The colour of the tile can also be enhanced through the firing process to create a brindle effect; the firing process also ensures that the tile colour is permanent. Clay tiles come in two main formats, the flatter plain tile and the larger format profiled tile.

Clay plain tiles can be laid to a minimum pitch of 35 degrees although you can purchase clay interlocking tiles that can be laid as shallow as 15 degrees. As with slates, there is a minimum head lap for plain clay tiles of 65mm. The minimum fixing specification for plain clay tiles is every fifth row; you may be required to improve the fixing method depending on wind loads.

Clay tiles are deemed to satisfy building regulations with respect to external fires. Interlocking clay tiles are now a very popular alternative; they require fewer tiles per square metre compared with using plain tiles and come in an array of colours, shapes and sizes.

CONCRETE ROOF TILES

Concrete Roof Tiles are probably the cheapest and most cost-effective roofing material. Concrete tiles are made from sand, water, cement and pigments then left to cure. Unlike clay tiles which are fired, they can usually be transported and laid just a few days after manufacture. One of the problems associated with concrete tiles is that the colour does tend to fade over a period of time.

With some types of concrete tiles you will only require 10 to 11 tiles to cover a square metre of roof, compared with around 60 plain clay tiles; this can be a large saving in both materials and labour. The life expectancy of a concrete roof tile is usually marketed at about 50 years.

THATCHED ROOF
A Thatched Roof, laid in a traditional way, will last up to 50 years. Although largely maintenance-free it is best to review a thatch annually. Thatched roofs provide a good level of insulation, purely by the nature of the material used in constructing the thatch. Thatched roofs are also aesthetically pleasing; they are becoming ever more popular as a roof covering on new build properties.

Thatching is a specialist trade - you may be faced with a long lead time when you choose to appoint a thatcher.

There are three main thatching materials:

Water Reed
Long Straw
Combed Wheat Reed

Others materials include Flax, Heather, Broom, Sods and Marram Grass.

Water reed is thought to be the most durable and will last up to 50 years.
If you are intending to use thatch, your roof structure will need to be designed accordingly; you can assume a weight of about 34 Kg/m2.

Thatched roofs are normally only found in certain areas of the country. In some conservation areas they may be a condition of planning approval.

First Fix

After your roofing work is complete you will be ready to start 'First Fixing' your property. First Fix means carrying out all necessary internal work, making it ready for plastering or dry lining. There is a set sequence of events when first fixing; you must also be aware of and comply with current Building Regulations.

Listed below are operations that need to be carried out as part of the First Fix:

- All staircases need to be fitted
- Plumbing pipe work needs to be installed
- Any internal soil stacks need to be fitted
- Floor needs laying (if you are having underfloor heating, insulation along with heating loops need laying and the floor will need to be screeded)
- All internal walls need erecting
- All noggins to carry plaster board need fixing (Additional noggins may be required in the kitchen area to allow a secure fixing for hanging wall units)
- All external doors and windows require fitting
- Window boards require fixing
- Any areas where the walls have been penetrated, for example floor joists and soil vent pipes, will need pointing with mortar, mastic or foam. This is important. When the house is complete you will need to carry out an air test. (Once your dwelling is plastered you will be unable to get back to some of these areas).
- All wiring will need to be installed, including the back boxes

STAIRS

There are many designs of stairs and some are beautifully crafted and can almost be treated as a piece of furniture, so it is important that when you place an order for your stairs it complies with current building regulations and you have given your chosen manufacturer all the correct dimensions. Finished floor height to finished floor height is one of the critical measurements that will be required.

Stairs must comply with Part K of the Building Regulations. Each individual riser should not exceed 220mm and the minimum length of a tread (known as the going) should not exceed 220mm. The pitch of a domestic stair case should not exceed 42 degrees. The width and length of every landing should be at least as great as the smallest width of the flight of stairs. Doors which swing across a landing at the bottom of a flight of stairs should leave a clear space of at least 400mm across the full width of the flight of stairs.

There should be 2.0m minimum headroom measured vertically above the pitch line of the stairs and landings, as indicated below:

HEADROOM FOR NEW STAIRS

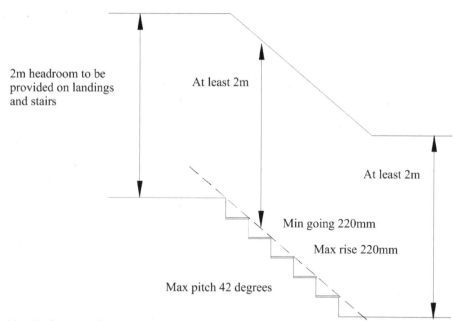

2m headroom to be provided on landings and stairs

At least 2m

At least 2m

Min going 220mm

Max rise 220mm

Max pitch 42 degrees

Handrails on staircases need to be 900mm above the pitch line. There needs to be at least one handrail to the side of the stairs. If stairs are wider than 1m then handrails will be required on both sides of the stairs. Ensure there is a clear width between handrails - a minimum of 600mm. Balustrading should be designed so it is unclimbable and should contain no space through which a 100mm sphere could pass. Ensure all flights of stairs have been structurally designed. Tapered treads and winders have the 'going' measured in the centre of the tread.

The minimum going of tapered treads, measured at the narrow end, is 50mm. Once your stairs are fitted it is best practice to cover and protect them to avoid any damage.

FIRST FIX PLUMBING

Before your chosen plumbing contractor can start work on site you will have to decide upon the type of heating and hot water system you are going to use. In addition you must have all relevant information available before first fix plumbing can commence.

The types of heating system required will be based on availability of the fuel type and system requirements.

The usual choices of fuel are gas, oil, electric or solid fuel. You will also need to decide if the system is to be supported by solar thermal or any other sustainable source.

Instantaneous systems (combination boilers) produce hot water on demand, but generally at significantly lower flow rates than storage systems. They should only be used where the simultaneous demand for hot water is limited, e.g. in homes with only one bathroom or shower room, unless you can find a manufacturer that can supply you with a boiler that is capable of producing hot water simultaneously to multiple outlets.

Standard boilers with a hot water storage capacity is the more common choice for larger properties. Most hot water storage vessels incorporate a fully pumped system which alleviates the need for cold water storage in loft spaces.

Minimum hot water storage should be as follows:

Home with a shower only - 60 litres storage

Home with a bath only - 120 litres storage

Home with a bath and shower - 145 litres storage

Home with two baths - 180 litres storage

Your plumbing contractor will need positions, types and sizes of the following:

Boiler
Hot Water storage
Cold Water tanks (if required)
Radiators
Towel rails
Domestic appliances
Gas Hob
Gas Fires
Sanitary ware
Showers
Outside taps

Even though positions may be indicated on your working drawings, your desired positioning of some of the above items often may differ. You will usually have a more comprehensive kitchen layout which will be a better guide for the plumbing contractor.

Soil and vent pipe routes and the installation of them needs to be undertaken at the first fix stage.

The type of floor joist used and pipe work to be installed will determine at what point the floors can be laid. If you are using engineered floor joists your flooring will have been laid at the same time as the joists were fitted. If you are using solid timber joists then it is likely that the plumber will need to notch the tops of the joists to allow him to lay his pipe work. Nowadays plastic pipe is common and because of its flexible nature allows for pipe work to be installed after the flooring is laid, unlike copper pipe which is more rigid and needs to be laid in straight runs.

INTERNAL WALLS
All internal structural walls will have been built at the same time as the super-structure; all the other internal walls that are required will only act as partitions, dividing the floor area into rooms. They are usually of a lightweight construction and are likely to be made from timber or lightweight metal.

Partitions should be built from a doubled up joist where partitions run parallel, or noggins should be provided where partitions run at right angles. Where partitions are built directly on a concrete slab they should be sat on DPC. The thickness of plaster board you are going to use affects the required spacings of the studs. If 9.5mm boards are to be used then the maximum stud spacing is 450mm. If you are using boards of a thickness between 10mm and 20mm then your maximum stud spacing is 600mm. Building Regulations for new build houses now require a downstairs cloakroom to allow disabled access: below is a sketch showing the minimum requirements.

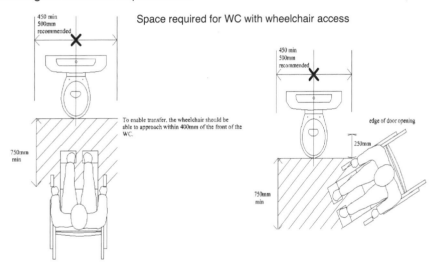

Space required for WC with wheelchair access

When constructing your partitions make sure your door openings comply with Part M of the Building Regulations. Part M covers 'Access and Facilities for disabled use'. It requires that in all new homes there should be a minimum clear width and a maximum threshold height for the principle entrance of the dwelling; this is usually considered to be the front door. This is to provide easy access to those in wheelchairs. The required clear opening width is at least 775mm. This is measured between the door stile and the face of the door when it is open at 90 degrees. This minimum requirement corresponds to a door 33 inches (919mm) wide, which would typically be 6ft 6ins high.

NOGGINS
Noggins need to be fixed to carry the edges of plasterboard. Additional noggins

are sometimes required to provide a solid fixing for kitchen wall units, radiators, bathroom units, sanitary ware and electrical back boxes.

EXTERNAL DOORS AND WINDOWS

Before the fitting of doors and windows you must make sure that insulated cavity closers are in place. Most closers will act as a vertical damp which is a requirement; otherwise you will need to vertically fix DPC to the side of all door and window frames. Windows and doors are usually fitted by the use of metal straps which are fixed to the outsides of the frames, protruding inwards so they can be fixed to the window reveals. Ensure all windows and doors are fitted level and plumb. Fixings should be no more than 600mm apart and not more than 150mm from the top or bottom. Make sure all frames are sealed after installation. Material that is intended to be painted should be primed before installation.

WINDOW BOARDS

Window boards should be primed and undercoated before being fitted. Most window boards slot into a groove or channel of the window frame. A preferred fixing method is by the use of holding down straps which are screwed to the underside of the window board protruding downwards. Allow for the straps to be fixed to the internal block work or timber. In the case of timber-framed dwellings, this prevents filling any screw holes at a later date.

Inspection
MAKE SURE your pre-plaster inspection is satisfactorily signed off before you commence any plastering

PRE-PLASTER INSPECTION

Once you have fully completed your First Fix you will need to have a pre-plaster inspection carried out by local building control and your warranty provider. They will check that all the work carried out up to that point is compliant with current Building Regulations. All roof bracings and restraint straps will also be inspected along with the first fixing. If there are any issues that the inspectors feel require attention, a re-visit may be required. It is important any issues are attended to and properly signed off as it could affect the issuing of your structural Warranty at the end of your project.

POINTING

Point with mortar or mastic all joist ends around window and door frames, under window boards and around all pipe that protrudes through the external walls. Sometimes,

where there are larger gaps, expanding foam is used. This operation is of the upmost importance as you will need the property to be correctly sealed to prevent air leakage; once plastering is complete you will be unable to access most of these areas.

WIRING

Next, all wiring and fixing back boxes needs to be done. Your electrical contractor will be aware of what is involved in an electrical first fix.

Make sure you have all the listed information in place:

All socket positions

Kitchen layout showing appliance positions

All lighting positions including wall lights, ceiling light,

external lights and any kitchen pelmet lighting

Required positions of all heating controls

Required positions of TV outlets

Telephone points

Alarms that you may require

CCTV

Any home entertainment system, including speakers

All electrical work needs to meet the requirements of Part P (electrical safety) and must be designed, installed, inspected and tested by a competent person, registered under a competent person self-certification scheme such as:

BRE Certification Ltd
BSI
NICEIC Certification services
Zurich Ltd

An appropriate BS7671 Electrical Installation Certificate will be required for the work and a copy will need to be given to Building Control on completion.

When deciding upon choosing windows for your new dwelling there are many issues that need to be taken into consideration as listed below:

- Planning
- Building Regulations
- Means of escape
- Ventilation
- Design for cleaning safely
- Maintenance
- Security
- Installation
- Glazing

PLANNING
Window styles and the materials used in the manufacturing of them may be subject to planning approval, especially if you are building in a conservation area. It is not uncommon for planning departments to specify timber frames, as opposed to the more common choice of UPVC frames in new dwellings.

If your window style needs to be approved with the local planning department ensure any conditions are satisfactorily met and signed off before you place any orders.

BUILDING REGULATIONS
Building regulations covering all aspects of windows can be found in the follow Approved Documents:

Approved Document A – Structure
Approved Document B – Fire Safety
Approved Document C – Resistance to Contaminants and Moisture
Approved Document F – Ventilation
Approved Document J – Combustion Appliances and Fuel Storage Systems
Approved Document K – Protection from Falling, Collision and Impact
Approved Document L – Conservation of Fuel and Power
Approved Document M – Access to and Use of Buildings
Approved Document N – Safety against Impact

Windows

MEANS OF ESCAPE

A fire escape window is required on the ground floor in any habitable room that does not open onto a hall leading directly to an exit door.

A fire escape window is required on upper floors not more than 4.5m above ground level in all habitable rooms (unless the room has direct access to a protected stairway). Upper floors more than 4.5m above ground level should be accessed by a protected stairway or an alternative escape route and therefore fire escape windows are not required.

There is no requirement to have more than one escape window in a room.
A fire escape window should have an unobstructed openable area that is at least 0.33m2 and at least 450mm high or 450mm wide. If one of the dimensions is 450mm minimum then the other dimension will need to be at least 734mm to achieve 0.33m2. The route through the window maybe at an angle rather than straight through the bottom, the opening area should be no more than 1100mm above the floor. The window should enable the person escaping to reach a place free from danger of fire.

VENTILLATION

There should be adequate means of ventilation provided for people inside the building; the target for new dwellings is four air changes per hour.

There are two types of ventilation that are required in a building

1 – Purge Ventilation which is required to remove high levels of pollutants and water vapour. It may also improve thermal comfort and reduce overheating during the summer months.

Requirements for Purge Ventilation via windows are as follows: For hinged or pivot windows that open 30 degrees or more, or for sliding sash windows, the area of the opening should be at least 1/20th of the floor area of the room. For a hinged or pivot window that opens less than 30 degrees, the area of the opening should be at least 1/10th of the floor area of the room.The opening areas for all windows in a room can be added together for the above purpose.

BUILD YOUR OWN
HOUSE

2 – Background Ventilation is important to allow a building to constantly 'breathe'. Good air quality is important for health and also protects the fabric of the building from harmful effects of condensation and mould etc. Background ventilation helps achieve this.

The usual method of achieving background ventilation is by having trickle vents fitted into the window frames.

DESIGN FOR CLEANING SAFELY
Under CDM (Construction Design and Management) all new properties need to be designed ensuring a safe method of window cleaning can be undertaken. One innovation that is worth considering is easy clean hinges for the upstairs windows; these hinges are designed to operate as a normal hinge, allowing cleaning of the external glass surface when opened from the inside.

MAINTENANCE
Good quality windows will give you years of trouble-free service. However regular maintenance will prolong the life of many of the components.

SECURITY
Hinges and fastenings of open lights of windows should be of a type which prevents them from being opened from the outside when in the closed position.

Opening lights on all ground floor windows and others which are readily accessible from the outside may be fitted with lockable devices which cannot be released without a key.

INSTALLATION
When fixing windows always follow manufacturers' instructions. There are two main principals for fixing windows:

Straps - Fixed to the sides of the frame and protruding into the window reveal. The straps can be fixed securely to the window reveal.

Screw and plug – Where the frames can be fixed directly to the window reveal through the frame.

All fixings should be corrosion-resistant and suitable to rigidly fix windows in place.

Prior to installation of your windows ensure all cavity closers and vertical DPC is correctly in place. Below are sections showing the correct methods:

WINDOW REVEAL

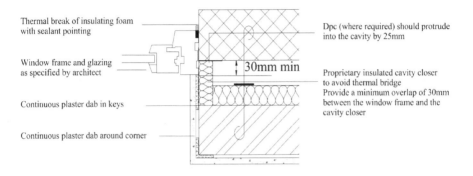

Thermal break of insulating foam with sealant pointing

Window frame and glazing as specified by architect

Continuous plaster dab in keys

Continuous plaster dab around corner

30mm min

Dpc (where required) should protrude into the cavity by 25mm

Proprietary insulated cavity closer to avoid thermal bridge
Provide a minimum overlap of 30mm between the window frame and the cavity closer

ROOFLIGHTS (SECTION)
Rooflight installed in accordance with manufacturers details

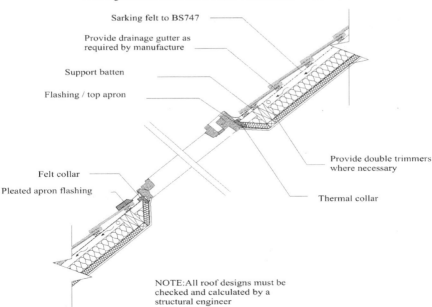

Sarking felt to BS747

Provide drainage gutter as required by manufacture

Support batten

Flashing / top apron

Felt collar

Pleated apron flashing

Provide double trimmers where necessary

Thermal collar

NOTE:All roof designs must be checked and calculated by a structural engineer

BUILD YOUR OWN
HOUSE

Fixing distances – where possible all four sides of the frame should be secured as follows:

- Corner fixings should be between 150mm and 250mm from the external corners
- No fixing should be less than 150mm from the centre line of the mullion or transom
- Intermediate fixings should be at centres no greater than 600mm
- There should be a minimum of two fixings on each jamb. If the head is fixed with polyurethane foam, then the fixings at the head may be as follows:
- Frame width up to 1200mm – no fixings
- Frame width 1201mm to 2400mm – one fixing
- Frame width 2401mm to 3600mm – two equally spaced fixings.

Installation packers should be used adjacent to fixing positions to prevent outer frame distortion during installation. Installation packers should be resistant to compression, rot and corrosion. They should span the full depth of the outer frame. The fixings should be tightened so that the frame is held securely against the packers. Over-tightening can lead to distortion and should be avoided. Where enhanced security is required, additional packers might be necessary adjacent to hinge and locking points. It is important that all windows are fitted plumb and square.

GLAZING

The correct glazing is critical to the overall energy performance of your new dwelling. Windows have their own labelling system known as Window Energy Rating (WER), an A rating on the scale being the most efficient. The thermal insulation properties of Low E double glazing achieves by far the best Window Energy Rating, and depending on their construction can obtain an A rating. Low E glass or low-emissivity glass has a transparent metallic oxide coating which acts like a one-way thermal gateway. The coating works by selectively reflecting long wave radiation, characteristic of internal heating sources. Solar heat gain, which is short-wave energy, can pass through into the room but indoor heating cannot escape to the outside as it is long-wave energy. The coating effectively reflects the rooms radiated heat back in, whilst allowing heat and light from the sun to enter through.

Windows

Safety glazing should be provided to any critical area. Below is a list giving guidance as to when safety glazing is required:

- Any glazed area within a window below 800mm from floor level
- Any glazed area within a window that is 300mm or less from a door and up to 1500mm from floor level.
- Within any glazed door up to 1500mm from floor level.

It is a legal requirement that the marking on the safety glass remains visible after installation. More information on safety glazing can be found in the Building Regulations Approved Document N.

Installing double glazed units – Not all windows are delivered pre glazed and it is always advisable to have double glazed units fitted by a suitably qualified person. In all cases the manufacturer's instructions should be followed. Insulating glass units should be installed in accordance with BS 8000-7 requiring, where appropriate, the correct use of setting blocks, distance pieces, frame to glass and bead to glass gaskets, bead to frame air seals, corner sealing blocks, beads and bead end caps and bedding and capping sealants.

WINDOW SILL

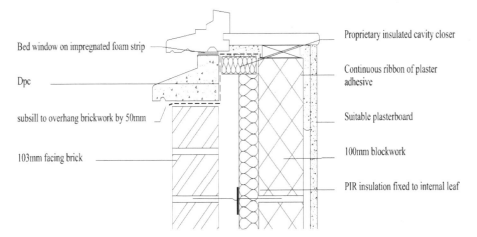

Bed window on impregnated foam strip

Dpc

subsill to overhang brickwork by 50mm

103mm facing brick

Proprietary insulated cavity closer

Continuous ribbon of plaster adhesive

Suitable plasterboard

100mm blockwork

PIR insulation fixed to internal leaf

Plastering, Dry Lining and Rendering is a coating primarily to get walls and ceilings to a standard ready for decoration. Plastering also incorporates many design issues and the correct materials should always be used.

The following points need to be considered before plastering can commence:

- Fire Resistance
- Thermal Insulation
- Sound Insulation

FIRE RESISTANCE
Requirements for providing areas of buildings that need to be resistant to fire can be found in the Building Regulation Approved Document B. Compliance is mandatory.
There are various methods of providing fire protection; the easiest option is by using the correct fire-resistant plasterboards. The main areas that require protection are any stairwells that are to a height of over 4.5m. Regulations require you to ensure the whole stairwell is resistant to fire for 30 minutes. The construction of integral garages also requires that they are resistant to fire for a minimum of 30 minutes.

THERMAL INSULATION
Working drawings that have been approved by building control should have all insulation requirements indicated.
There is sometimes a requirement to introduce additional Thermal Insulation to the external walls of a new dwelling after the Superstructure is complete. If your dwelling is of a timber construction suitable insulation will be placed between the studs of the timber frame. If your external wall construction is of the more traditional masonry construction then you will probably be looking at using insulated plasterboard. Insulated plasterboard comes in a variety of thicknesses and will reduce your room sizes, so you must take in to consideration the use of insulated plasterboard at the design stage.

There are two methods of fixing insulated plasterboard. You can mechanically fix the boards to a metal or timber framework or you can directly board onto the masonry using an adhesive bonding known as 'Dot and Dab'.

Integral garage ceilings will require suitable insulation; this can normally be achieved by using Quilt insulation.

There are many products now on the market to achieve your required level of insulation.

The most common types of insulation are:

- Insulated plasterboard
- Multi Layered foil insulations
- Quilt insulation

Garages

Walls between integral garages and the main dwelling are considered to be external walls and will need to be insulated accordingly.

SOUND INSULATION

Sound Insulation is sometimes required to improve the acoustic performance of a dwelling. If your new dwelling has a party wall then you will need to achieve a level of sound insulation. There is a variety of methods that can be used to help you achieve this. A combination of the following may be required to achieve the necessary acoustic wall construction.

- Parge coating
- Cavity insulation
- Insulated plasterboard

All newly-constructed dwellings that incorporate party walls need to comply with the Building Regulations Approved Document E.
To satisfy building control of compliance, you can either construct your dwelling in accordance with a Robust Detail which needs to be purchased directly from Robust Details or you can have your dwelling tested for the Acoustic Performance on completion.

Other areas of a newly-constructed dwelling where sound insulation should be considered are as follows:

- Downstairs Ceilings
- Soil pipe boxings
- Partition walls from bathrooms and cloakrooms.

The usual method of achieving sound insulation is by using Sound Block Plasterboard or Fibre Quilt.

Methods of Internal Plastering, Dry Lining and Rendering

Internal Plastering – Nowadays the most common method of internal plastering is to clad all the internal walls and ceilings with plasterboard and then apply a skimmed plaster finish.

You must ensure that the plasterboard selected is correct for its use, i.e. sound block and fire wall plasterboards should be fixed in the appropriate areas.

Plasterboard fixed to metal or timber stud walls will usually be fixed by nails or screws. Always use fixings that are recommended. Plasterboard that is fixed to masonry can be stuck on using Dry-Wall Adhesive, the 'Dot and Dab' method.

After all the boards are fixed in place the corners will require angle beads. All the joints will require plasterer's scrim; this will stop any cracking. Finally a plaster finish is applied and troweled to a smooth finish ready for decoration.

Dry Lining – The walls and ceilings should all be covered with plasterboard which is manufactured especially for dry lining. It still needs to comply with regulations for fire and sound. Angle beads will need to be fixed into position and all the joints taped and covered with a jointing compound. Once set the compound is rubbed down to leave a smooth and level finish. A plasterboard sealer or primer will then need to be applied prior to decoration.

External Render – The main things to be considered when choosing a suitable render for your project will be the finished texture and the colour.

There are many methods and materials that can be used to achieve textures and colours.

A natural render will be of the colour and texture of the aggregates used, which are usually a combination of sand and cement.

Silicone renders are now becoming more popular and come in an extensive range of textures and colours.

External finishes should always be approved by your local planning department and in some conservation areas you may have to use recommended methods. Before you can commence with any rendering operations you should have all your windows fitted and your scaffolds adapted accordingly.

It is always a good idea to have all guttering fitted with temporary downpipes to throw any water away from your walls.

Plastering and Rendering will form part of a finished look to a new property. When appointing a suitable contractor it is worth gaining references and maybe taking time to look at work they have previously completed.

BUILD YOUR OWN
HOUSE

When you have completed your internal plastering and have allowed a suitable time for it to dry, you will be ready to Second Fix your new property. A lot of thought will need to go into the choices you make for Second Fix materials, as they will collectively make up the look and style of the property. This is also the point when you need to have your gas and electric meters installed.

Items that make up a Second Fix are:

- Balustrades and Handrails
- Skirting Boards and Architraves
- Internal Doors
- Kitchen and Utility Areas
- Heating System
- Hot Water System
- Floor and Wall Tiling
- Wet Wall Boards
- Electrics
- Sanitary ware

Budgets
Beware! Budgets can easily run away with themselves when selecting material for your second fix

BALUSTRADES AND HANDRAILS
Balustrades and handrails have a primary function but can also be decorative, enhancing the look of the stairs and the grandeur of the property. A decision will have to be made if your staircase is of a timber construction.

You should decide whether to paint the stairs and stair parts or retain the natural wood and have them stained, waxed or varnished. If you intend not to paint them you should have them made from better quality timber. Hardwoods like oak are ideal but also costly.

Not all Balustrades are timber. Glass panels are very popular or perhaps you could consider using stainless steel and cable. The choices can be endless. The design of your stairs needs to be kept in line with the budget you will have set out.

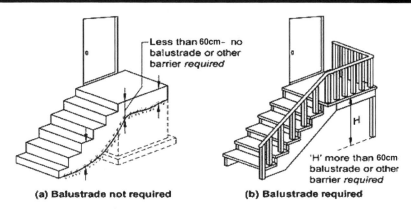

(a) Balustrade not required   **(b) Balustrade required**

Whatever type of balustrade and handrail you decide to fit these will still need to be compliant with building regulations as follows:

A handrail should be provided for any flight of stairs that rises 600mm or more. The hand rail should be fixed between 900mm (840mm in Scotland) and 1000mm vertically above the pitch line. The whole length of the handrail should be fixed securely, in a continuous line, smooth and unobstructed; it should be at least 25mm from any surface. You should check that fixings and locations are in accordance with design. All balustrades should be fixed securely, designed so that they cannot easily be climbed, with no gaps which could allow a 100mm diameter sphere to pass through.

SKIRTING BOARDS AND ARCHITRAVES

Skirting boards and architraves usually have matching mouldings. If you wish to go for a standard moulding your choices are normally limited to – Chamfered, Ogee, Half Round and Torus. If a different designed moulding is required good joinery workshops will be able to have cutters made so a desired moulding can be produced.

If you are intending to stain or varnish your skirtings and architraves make sure you use a suitable quality of timber. If they are to be painted then MDF can be used as an option to timber. Care should be taken when fixing architraves and skirtings, they must be fixed securely with adhesive and screws. If you are intending to stain or varnish your skirting and architraves once fitted you will need to countersink the screws and insert timber plugs made from the same timber.

BUILD YOUR OWN
HOUSE

INTERNAL DOORS

You may find that some of the internal doors have a requirement to be fire doors. This normally applies to doors that give direct access to a stairwell that is more than 4.5metres high. The casings (frames) or the doors will also need to have intumescent strips inserted. Intumescent is substance that swells to form a seal in the event of a fire. A fire door would also be required if you have a door opening into an integral garage.

Always ensure the correct door casings are fitted, check the door's width and height, and ensure that the rebates on the frames are correct to receive the doors.

Ensure the doors are of the correct width to allow for disabled access as required by Building Regulations - guidance can be found in:

Approved Document Part M.

KITCHEN AND UTILITY

Your kitchen and utility layouts should be prepared on the commencement of construction on site. This will ensure that all drainage, gas, electric and water connections are located in the correct positions before the kitchen and utility items arrive on site. You don't want to be moving any drainage or pipe work after your kitchen has been fitted.

Before you actually purchase your kitchen and utility, check all dimensions of the kitchen and utility areas and make sure all electrics and pipework are in the correct position.

Ensure all appliance spaces are of the correct dimensions, as appliance sizes greatly differ.

Most good kitchen companies will plan your kitchen in accordance with your working drawings. This service is often free of charge, but it is likely the kitchen company will require a form of commitment for carrying out this service.

Here is a typical kitchen plan:

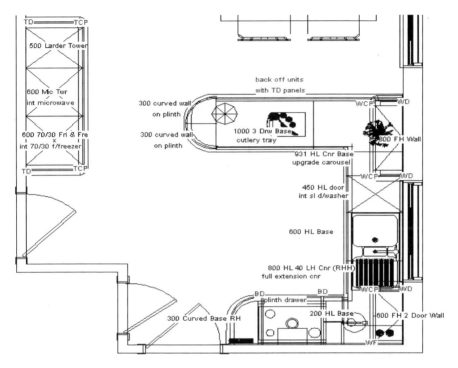

Some kitchen companies provide a supply and fit service, which is normally the best option as it puts the onus on the kitchen company to correctly install all the units and ensure they are undamaged. If a supply and fit route is one you going down then ensure you give your self time to properly inspect checking for any damage before you sign for it as complete. You will find it difficult to fight your case for something like a scratched worktop if it hasn't been recorded before you have signed it off as satisfactory.

If you are buying your kitchen on a supply only basis, you will need to employ a kitchen fitter; some site joiners/carpenters do install kitchens, but it is usually best to use a tradesman that specialises in fitting kitchens. Worktops also come in a range of colours, sizes and material. It is not uncommon to purchase your worktops from a different source than the kitchen units themselves, especially if you are planning to have granite or marble work surfaces fitted. These products will be made and fitted by specialists.

HEATING SYSTEM

Your heating system will have been designed according to the type of fuel you are going to use; this decision will have been made and put into place at the design stage.

By the Second Fix stage of the build you will have decided upon your heating system and all the pipework should have been installed at the First Fix stage. Regardless of the type of fuel you are using most boilers have a SEDBUK (Seasonal Efficiency of Domestic Boilers in the UK) rating on a scale of 1 – 100; the higher the number the greater the efficiency. You should always try and install the most efficient boiler available.

All heating systems have to comply with Building Regulation Approved Document Part L, Conservation of Fuel and Power in new dwellings. The Part L Approved Document requires that reasonable provisions are made to conserve fuel and power. Part of this is achieved by installing fuel-efficient boilers with effective controls. Heating controls should include thermostatic radiator valves, zone controls and suitable boiler programmers.

Generally, all dwellings with a floor area over 150m2 should have at least two space heating zones.

You must make sure that when positioning your boiler the flue, where terminated externally, is positioned a minimum of 600mm away from any door or window openings.

HOT WATER SYSTEM

Most domestic hot water systems are connected to the primary heat source, usually a boiler. Hot water can be supplemented with additional systems; examples being, solar thermal or electric. It is important that effective controls are fitted to enable water always to be heated by the most cost-effective and environmentally-friendly source. For example, should Solar Thermal be the primary source for hot water, it will need to be backed up from another source (especially in the UK).

To ensure your heating and hot water systems comply, there is a HM Government publication available titled "Domestic Building Service Compliance Guide".

FLOOR AND WALL TILING

Floor and wall tiling needs to be carried out at the Second Fix stage. These will have an impact on other Second Fix operations to be carried out.

It may sound obvious but, **never** use wall tiles on floors.

In rooms that are having floor tiles laid you should delay fitting any skirting boards until the tiling operation is complete; then the skirting boards should be fixed securely on top of the tiling. This will give a much neater appearance.

If doors are to open over the tiling allowances should be made for the thickness of the tiles. This is only applicable where doors are hung before the tiling is laid. It is not normal to tile underneath kitchen units, baths and shower trays, so these can be fitted prior to floor tiling. You have to make sure that you tile far enough under kitchen units and baths so that any plinths or bath panels will sit on top of the tiles.

Wall tiling is generally carried out in bathrooms, en-suites, cloakrooms and kitchens. If bathroom walls are to be fully tiled it is advisable to fix toilets and basins in place then remove them to allow for tiling to commence. This will ensure that any pipes where tiles need to be cut around are in the correct positions. If tiling is for splash backs and shower areas only, then all sanitary ware can be fixed first.

Fixing of floor tiles – this can be directly on to solid floors, but you must first ensure the floors are flat and level. Use a floor levelling compound where necessary.

When fixing floor tiles to a timber floor you should first cover the tiled area with 6mm WBP ply, screwed every 150mm. On timber floors flexible floor adhesives and grouts should be used.

When fixing wall tiles always use the correct size beading suitable for the tiles. Good tile retailers will ensure they supply you the correct size beading.

When tiling is carried out in wet areas, ensure all adhesives and grouts are suitably waterproof and mould-resistant. When purchasing wall or floor tiles always ensure they are fit for their intended use.

WET WALL BOARDS
Wall boards are becoming increasingly more common, especially in bath and shower rooms, where they are seen as an alternative to tiles.
Wall boards have a WBP plywood core and a laminated surface that comes in a large selection of finishes. They are supplied with internal and external trims. One of the advantages of using wall boards is that they are much quicker to install, which can reduce labour costs.

ELECTRICS
All electrical work carried out on your new dwelling including wiring, installation and all associated components, has to be compliant with building regulations and electrical safety as found in Approved Document P.

Before your electrician can begin a Second Fix you will have to choose the style of your plug sockets and light switches. There are plenty on the market to choose from, e.g. chrome, brass, brushed steel and plastic, you will find numerous designs available on the market. It is always a good idea to take advice from a registered electrician before purchasing any fittings to ensure they comply with all current regulations. If electricians deem any components as non-compliant they will not fit them, as they will be issuing the Electrical Certificate.

Second Fix electrics will include installation of the following:
Fitting all plug sockets
Fitting all light switches
Installation of the consumer unit and connecting to the mains
Installing all light fittings

Fitting TV and any media sockets
Installing burglar alarms
Outside lighting
Installation of all heating and hot water controls
Any CCTV that may be required

Internal and external lighting for all new dwellings must meet relevant energy efficiency requirements as follows:

For fixed internal lighting you must provide low energy light fittings not less than three per four (Excluding infrequently accessed spaces used for storage, such as cupboards and wardrobes).

Low energy light fittings should have lamps with a luminous efficacy greater than 45 lamp lumens per circuit-watt and a total output greater than 400 lamp lumens. Light fittings whose supplied power is less than 5 circuit-watts are excluded from overall count of the total number of light fittings.

Where external lighting is installed, provide light fittings with the following characteristics:

(A)   Either

1-   Lamp capacity not greater than 100 lamp-watts per light fitting

2-   All lamps automatically controlled to switch off after the area lit by the fitting becomes unoccupied

3-   All lamps automatically controlled to switch off when daylight is sufficient

(B)   Or:

1 -   Lamp efficacy greater than 45 lumens per circuit-watt

2 -   All lamps automatically controlled to switch off when daylight is sufficient

3-   Light fittings controllable manually by the occupants

SANITARY WARE

Sanitary ware is a personal choice and you will find numerous suppliers, but you must ensure that you comply with the Building Regulation Approved Document Part G, which covers water efficiency. This sets out that all new dwellings need to be designed to achieve a projected water consumption of less than 125 litres per person per day (or much lower for Code for Sustainable Homes dwellings).

At the design stage you will need to have completed *Part G Water Calculations* which will be based on the floor plans and an understanding of the fittings you are installing.

Some of the issues that water calculation addresses are: the measurement of tap flowrates, bathtub sizes and toilet flush volumes, as well as rainwater and greywater systems.

Discharges
All water discharged from sanitary ware must be directed into the foul drainage system

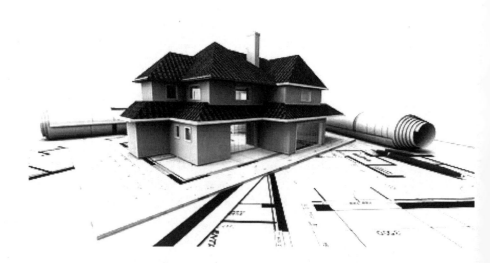

Decorating is an operation that is sometimes carried out by the self-builder. However maintaining a high quality finish is a more skilful operation to undertake than is given credit for.

If you are not planning to undertake the decoration then you will have to engage a decorator. Smaller one man band decorators are usually happy to carry out the work on a supply and fix basis. Alternatively they can supply you with the labour, in which case you purchase the materials yourself. Larger decorating companies will prefer to supply the labour and the materials.

All painting and decorating, including all material used, should be in accordance with **'BS 6150 'Code of Practise for painting of buildings'.**

If any coving is required it should be put in place before any painting commences. It is often the job of a decorator to fit coving although this is sometimes carried out by plastering contractors. In the case of timber coving this would be fixed by a carpenter/joiner.

Coving is available in an array of depths, patterns and materials. Certain types of coving are suited to certain types of property.

Calculating the amount of paint required will depend on the paint and the paint manufacturer. Below is a rough guide to the coverage you can expect:

1 litre of emulsion will cover approximately 12 to 14 square metres
of internal walls and ceilings
1 litre of acrylic undercoat will cover approximately 13 square metres
1 litre of acrylic gloss will cover approximately 10 square metres

Most cans of paint will have the coverage indicated on them.

Preparation is the key to a good finish, often taking far longer than the actual paint application process.

Next is a list of surface preparation prior to painting:

- Ensure all plaster surfaces are visibly sound
- Fill and rub down any nail holes, cracks or any other surface imperfections
- All surfaces should be free from dirt, dust or any moisture
- All door furniture should be removed
- Surfaces to be stained or varnished should be prepared to provide adequate adhesion.
- Fill or caulk along the tops of skirtings and architraves, where necessary
- Apply any stabilising treatments that may be recommended
- One full round coat of primer should be applied to all surfaces to be painted, and to hidden surfaces of external woodwork

When purchasing paint for wood and metal work you will find there is a choice between water-based and oil-based products.

Oil-based products have a longer dry time but will give a more attractive gloss finish but are not as environmentally-friendly as they contain more VOC's (volatile organic compounds). Brushes will also need cleaning with a mineral spirit, which is not as environmentally-friendly to dispose of. Water-based products are low in VOC's, easier to clean brushes with water, they have a quicker drying time and the colour is considered to be more stable over time without yellowing.

Decorating structural steel – All steelwork should be protected against corrosion by using protective paints that comply with **BS EN ISO 12944.** Internal and external steelwork which hasn't been galvanised should be protected by at least two coats of zinc phosphate primer and a suitable decorative finish where required.

If steel work is to be protected by intumescent paint, then manufacturer's guide lines should be followed. Intumescent paint, in the event of a fire, expands up to 50 times the paint film thickness to form an insulating char layer. The char keeps the steel below a critical temperature to maintain the structural stability of the building.

BUILD YOUR OWN
HOUSE

Wallpapering may be required to all walls or just a feature wall. If so ensure you seal the walls that are to receive the wallpaper. To seal or size a wall you should apply a weak mix of paste. If you are painting any external masonry walls, ensure the walls have had sufficient time to dry. Always use suitable masonry paint. Good masonry paint contains algicide and fungicide to protect the paint film from staining due to mould, algal and fungal growth. Masonry paint also needs to be UV resistant.

Wood stains and varnishes are an alternative to paint and will enhance the look of the wood whilst giving them a protective coating. If your intended finish is going to be a stain or a varnish then you should ensure the wood quality and its fixing method is of a high standard.

FINAL FIX

After all decorating is complete and fully dry you are ready to commence with your final fix. Final fix will include the following:

- The fixing of all door handles, locks, door closers and any bolts required
- Installing loft hatches and loft ladders if required. Loft hatches must comply with the Code of Practice for design of the air tightness of ceilings.
- The air leakage rate through the frame should be less than 1.0m3/hr at a pressure of 2Pa.
- Loft hatch lids should also be thermally insulated to comply with Approved Document Part L Conservation of Fuel and Power.
- Fix all doorstops and door restrictors. Fix all intumescent strips that may be required to fire doors and frames.
- Fixing of draft excluders to all external doors and windows, with UVPC doors and windows draft excluders and seal usually come factory fitted.

Loft Insulation – Your building regulation drawings will indicate which insulation is required. There are many types of loft insulation on the market. When insulating loft spaces you will need to comply with current building regulations ensuring all insulation materials achieve a minimum of 0.20 W/m2K. If you are insulating an empty loft space directly onto the ceiling and you are intending to use glass mineral wool insulation, then it will need to be a minimum 270mm thick.

12.L
Decoration and Final Fix

Build Clean – there are cleaning companies that specialise in build cleans although you may decide to carry out this operation yourself. It is basically a case of getting rid of dust and dirt that has been created during the build process. Ensure all protective films are removed from windows, window frames, sanitary ware, kitchen units and worktops. It is important that cleaning is completed before any mastic pointing is carried out.

Mastic Pointing – There are plenty of companies that specialise in mastic pointing or you can have a go yourself. However it is not as easy as it looks and as it is a finished product that is on show it needs to have a neat appearance.

There are many different types of mastics with a good range of colours on the market; you must ensure the correct mastic is used for its designed function.

Listed are the areas that will need mastic sealants applied:

Around the ceiling edge of an integral garage will require an intumescent sealant

Around all window frames externally (unless there's an external render)

Around baths, showers and basins

Along the back edge of kitchen worktops

Appliances – All domestic appliances should be installed by suitably qualified tradesmen. Take care to retain all literature that comes with the new appliances and register them if required. Inspect them for any signs of damage, making sure that they work correctly; try and do this as soon as they have been installed.

A lot of thought needs to go into planning the layout of all external areas; you must endeavour to get the best use out of the area you have to work with. It would be nice to think you could accommodate everything you wish, but with outside space sometimes limited hard choices may be required. There will obviously be some external features that you will not be able to eliminate, access being the main one, but take into account your future requirements for outside living, designing private and secluded areas.

Listed are the main points and possible requirements that will need to be taken into consideration when designing your outside space:

- Driveways
- Paths
- Garages and Carports
- Sheds and Outbuilding
- Boundary Walls and Fences
- Conservatories
- Timber Decking
- Swimming Pools
- Hot Tubs etc
- Landscaping

DRIVEWAYS

When designing your driveways there will be building control and Highway requirements that you will need to satisfy. You will normally find that at the planning stage a copy of your application will have been sent to the highway department for comment making sure it complies with highway standards.
Visibility splays will be assessed. A visibility splay should be provided for vehicles

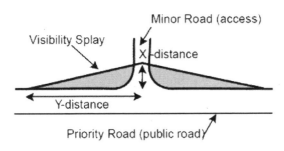

There should be an unobstructed view over all parts of the shaded area at a height of 1.05 metres above ground level (this represents the normal driver's eye height) from point X. Point X is the centre line of the access road and the required distance back from the edge of the main road. This distance should be 2 metres for a single dwelling access and 2.4 metres for shared access.

Distance Y is based on the stopping distance in relation to the speed at which the vehicle is likely to be travelling. This distance would usually refer to the main carriageway speed limit at the point of access.

Speed(mph)	Distance Metres. Y
30	90
40	120
50	160
60	215
70	295

Drives serving only one dwelling should have a width not less than 2.7 metres. Shared private drives should have a minimum width of 4.25 metres, so as to allow two vehicles to pass in the entrance without obstructing the road and to allow for any parked cars in the drive. Any walls along the length of the drive should be set back 0.5 metres.

The gradient of a drive should not exceed 1:20 for the first 5 metres from the highway boundary; this distance should be measured from the back of the footpath or verge, not edge of the road. Off street parking should be provided within the site, dwellings with 3 or less bedrooms will require a minimum of 2 parking spaces and dwellings with 4 or more bedrooms will require a minimum of 3 parking spaces. In all cases one or more parking spaces may be a garage. Where a minimum of 3 spaces is required you must be able to gain access to at least 2 spaces when the other is occupied.

On busy roads (generally with peak hour flows exceeding 300 vehicles/hour) it would be dangerous for cars to reverse out of the driveway onto the road. In this instance provisions should be made when laying your drive way to allow for

vehicles to turn and exit the driveway in a forward direction. All drives should be surfaced in hard bound material (not loose aggregate or gravel) for at least 5 metres behind the highway boundary.

Building regulations require that rainwater that runs off driveways isn't discharged onto the main highway or into the mains drainage system. You must disperse the water by either a permeable surface or a method of trapping the surface water and letting it soak away elsewhere on your property.

Before you start constructing your drive ensure that it is being constructed on stable ground and that all vegetation has been removed. It should be excavated to a depth which allows a suitable amount of sub-base material to be laid.

A good sub-base material would be MOT Type 1 sometimes referred to as DOT Type 1 it usually consists of granite or limestone with sizes ranging from 40mm down to dust. On stable ground this would be around 150mm deep. The sub-base should then be well compacted.

You will have to decide on your final driveway surface. The more common choice would be concrete – which will require to be laid to a minimum depth of 100mm.

Block paving - For a private drive a minimum thickness of 50mm is required

Tarmacadam - This will require a binder course (base course) of a minimum of 60mm and a surface course (wearing course) of a minimum of 20mm.

Gravel - It is recommended that gravel is laid to a depth of between 25mm and 40mm.

When forming a new access onto a highway any work carried out outside your boundary will need to be undertaken by an approved contractor. County Councils divisional offices will be able to provide you with a list of approved contractors; work must not be carried out until relevant permits have been obtained.

PATHS

All new properties should have adequate access provided to the main and secondary doors. Paths should comply with relevant building regulations and also be in accordance with Approved Document Part M (Access To and Use of Buildings). Where disabled access may be required, ensure it is constructed to allow for wheelchairs.

Below is a typical section of a threshold which is compliant with disabled access:

THRESHOLD DETAIL

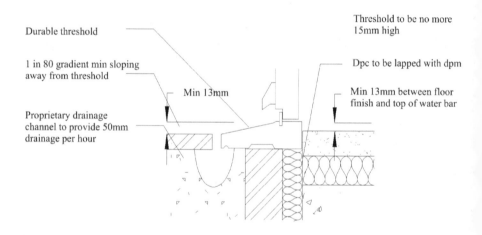

Durable threshold

Threshold to be no more 15mm high

1 in 80 gradient min sloping away from threshold

Dpc to be lapped with dpm

Min 13mm

Min 13mm between floor finish and top of water bar

Proprietary drainage channel to provide 50mm drainage per hour

If you are intending to have a garage or a carport then access should be provided to a main or secondary door.

Paths to the main entrance or any entrance that may be designated by building regulations must have a width of a minimum of 900mm.
Any paths that are used for refuse to a collection point must have a minimum width of 900mm. Paths that are adjoining a dwelling must have a minimum width of 700mm. Where paths are more than 100mm away from a dwelling they will require a minimum width of 600mm.

All other paths that may be required should have a minimum width of 600mm. Paths should not have any gradients that exceed 1:6. You may need to introduce steps to ensure maximum gradients are not exceeded.

If steps are required they should be constructed with a maximum rise of 220mm and a minimum going of 220mm. If any paths are adjacent to ground that has a drop more than 600mm then handrails must be provided; this also applies if the total rise of a flight of steps exceeds 600mm.

There are many different types of surface finishes for garden paths and it is totally an individual choice. Whatever finish you use in the construction of your paths ensure that it is laid on a well-consolidated sub-base. Paths around houses should be 150mm below the damp course, except for the areas where access into the dwelling is required.

GARAGES and CARPORTS

Usually garages and carports that are constructed within the boundary of the dwelling will not require planning permission as they are considered to be permitted development. This is subject to the following conditions:

- They are not constructed on any land that is forward of a wall forming the principal elevation
- They are to be single storey with a maximum eaves height of 2.5 metres and a maximum of 4 metres with duel pitched roofs, or 3 metres for any other roof
- No more than half the land around the main dwelling is covered by additions or other buildings

Building regulation approval is not normally required for a detached garage or carport if these guidelines are met:

- The floor area of a detached garage is less than 15 square metres
- The floor area of the garage is between 15 and 30 square metres; provided it is at least one metre from any boundary or it is constructed substantially from non-combustible materials.
- If a new garage is attached to the home then it will require Building Regulation approval.

Check with your Warranty provider to see if detached garages are included as part of the warranty. If they are then they may need to carry out stage inspections.

The construction process of garages is fairly similar to that of your main dwelling apart from the fact it is not required to have the same thermal performance as the main dwelling. All foundations, floor slabs and roofs still require to be structurally designed in accordance with relevant building regulations and statutory requirements. An inner leaf of wall construction to a detached garage will not be required. The garage floor slab should be laid with a fall allowing any water to be directed out of the main garage door.

You should provide adequate drainage to accommodate any rainwater. Garages should be constructed so they can be reasonable secure against unauthorised entry, which is very different from a car port that is left open on at least one side.

SHEDS AND OUTBUILDINGS
You will find a huge range of outbuildings and sheds available on the market - everything from standard garden sheds to fully-customised and kitted out garden offices. You will have to make your own choices - space and budget being the two main factors. Outbuildings and sheds will rarely require planning permission as they are considered to be permitted development, subject to certain limits very similar to garages.

If you are ever unsure it is always wise to make enquires at your local planning department before you commence with any construction or purchase.

BOUNDARY WALLS and FENCES
Boundary Walls are far more expensive to construct than the timber alternative, but are generally thought to be far more attractive and robust, providing they have been properly designed.
Depending on what part of the country you live in will depend on your choice of walling material as walls are normally designed to match their surroundings.
Natural stone, block and render or plain brick will be the most common types of walls that you will come across.

All boundary and freestanding walls need careful attention to design and specification. Design consideration will take into account the height in relation to horizontal forces, particularly wind.

Other design considerations would be:

- Copings should be considered to protect the top of the wall from the elements. An overhang should be provided to form a drip.
- The bottom of the foundation for all walls should be a minimum of 450mm below finished ground level
- Freestanding walls longer than 10 metres require movement joints to control expansion caused by changes in moisture content and temperature. There should be vertical joints breaking the wall up into discontinuous lengths to prevent cumulative stress that could cause cracking, movement or instability.
- If building any walls near trees then the foundations should be designed accordingly
- Piers should be introduced to walls to add strength particularly where gates are to be introduced

Timber fences will be a much cheaper option than a solid wall and there are plenty of choices on the market, the cheapest being post and rail; however it will not provide much in the way of security or privacy. A close boarded fence at a height of 1.8m with the posts concreted into the ground is the most common fencing you will see around new developments and, if correctly erected, you can expect a long lifespan.

If retaining walls are required always have them designed by a structural engineer. Retaining walls can be designed and constructed in many different ways but all have the same main objective of retaining ground between two different elevations.

If a retaining structure is required and will be more than 600mm high, then you will be required to place a handrail to the higher level.

CONSERVATORIES

Adding a conservatory to a dwelling is considered permitted development and does not normally require planning permission; there are limits and conditions which can be viewed on the Government planning portal.

Listed below are some of the conditions:
- No more than half the area of the land around the footprint of the original house is covered with extensions/conservatories
- No conservatories should be constructed forward of the principle elevation.
- Maximum height of a conservatory to be 4 metres
- There should be a maximum eaves height of 3 metres, if within 2 metres of the boundary

Conservatories are exempt from building regulations providing they comply with the following:
- They are built at ground level and are less than 30 square metres in floor area
- The conservatory is separated from the house by external quality walls, doors and windows
- There should be an independent heating system with separate temperature and on/off controls
- Glazing and any fixed electrical installations comply with the applicable building regulation requirements
- 75% of the roof must be transparent or translucent

It is important to remember that if you are planning having a non-separated conservatory, meaning that no external doors are present between the conservatory and the main dwelling then it will be considered as an extension. The design will then have to comply with building regulations and the construction will have to be inspected at various stages.

TIMBER DECKING

Timber Decking is getting ever more popular as an alternative to paved patio areas; Deck structures are not always exempt from planning permission.

Listed are situations where planning permission for decking is required:

- Where decking is situated within 20 metres of a highway
- Where the deck platform is more than 300mm from the ground
- Where the structure would affect the amenity value or privacy of neighbouring properties
- If Decking covers more than 50% of a property's garden

If planning permission is required it should also be assumed that building regulations will apply. If you are intending any timber decking to be included as part of a warranty, ensure it is designed to meet any service life requirements.

SWIMMING POOLS

Swimming Pools are classed in the same way as most outbuildings. Any structure that you use to cover the pool, providing it is of a single storey construction with a maximum eaves height of 2.5 metres and a maximum roof height of 4 metres, would not generally require planning permission.

There are many different methods to consider in constructing a swimming pool. It is best to engage a contractor dedicated to the installation of swimming pools, as they will be able to advise you on your personal requirements.
Ensure all your required features are incorporated into the design before any building work commences.

LANDSCAPING

Landscaping will add the finishing touch to any new property; it will be down to personal choice and available budget. However, there are a few points that should be observed:

- If topsoil needs to be imported ensure its source has been validated and it has an appropriate certificate when it is delivered. If the source cannot be proven it would be wise not to accept it.
- When planting any trees ensure they are planted far enough away from any structures, allowing for any impact they may have when fully grown
- Make sure all plants including trees, shrubs and grass are planted in the correct planting season

Not all meters and media connections are fitted at the same time as the incoming main supply is laid and there are certain procedures to be followed for meter installation. Additional information will be required to enable your gas and electric meters to be fitted.

WATER METERS

Waters meters are fitted at the same time that the incoming service pipe is made live by the water supply company.

Smart Meter
Where a smart meter is to be fitted you will need to have your gas meter already installed, if applicable

The Water meters will be fitted in one of three locations, which are as follows:

1 – Internally
2 – In-wall box
3 – Wall-mounted box

If your meter is to be installed inside the property then prior to your connection being made you will have to install a WRAS approved concentric meter adapter, which needs to be fitted directly above the internal stop tap, ready for the meter to be fixed. For all water supplies that have internal meters fitted, an underground control box must be installed as close to the front elevation as possible in a hard standing area to enable the water supply to be isolated if required.

Most suppliers of water now install meters equipped with the capability to be remotely read using Automated Meter Reading Technology (AMR). This means access to the property is not required to obtain a meter reading.

GAS METERS

The company that lays and connects a gas service to your property will not be the supplier of the gas that actually runs through the pipes. The gas company you use to connect your service pipe to the main will issue you with a MPRN. Every property that has a gas supply in the UK will have a MPRN (Meter Point Reference Number).

The MPRN will be allocated to your address and does not change if you change gas suppliers. The MPRN number is unique to each property. Your MPRN number should not be confused with your gas supplier's Account number. Once you have chosen your preferred supplier of gas, you will need to quote your MPRN number to enable them to fit a meter and supply gas to your property.

M.P.A.N.
Each MPAN must be registered with a supplier before a meter can be connected and final energisation can take place

ELECTRIC METERS
Once your electric service cable has been connected by the distribution company you will be able to apply for your meter. Electri cal distribution companies are not electrical supply companies.

The distribution company will provide you with a MPAN (Meter Point Administration Number). This is a unique number and will identify each electrical supply point.

You need to choose a preferred supplier for your electricity. Once chosen they will require the MPAN number to enable them to come and fix a meter and give you an electric supply.

SMART METERS
Smart meters communicate between gas and electric meters, measuring energy consumption in the same manner as a traditional meter but also allowing information to be read remotely. This is displayed to a device within the home, or the information can be read securely, externally. Smart meters will send meter readings to your energy supplier automatically. The device within your home is intended to give you up-to-date information about how much gas and electricity you are using. This can be read in units or pounds and pence.

The Government is planning for smart meters to be installed in every home in the UK by 2020. It is hoped that by installing smart meters it will lead to significant changes in how we use energy in the home. The meter itself will not reduce your usage, but will give you a better understanding of usage by displaying your energy consumption at different times of the day, week or month, suggesting ways that your energy consumption may be reduced.

Smart meters will be fitted by your chosen energy supplier at no extra cost. In design stages, if you are working to achieve a higher code for sustainable homes, a smart meter will gain you extra points.

If you have a smart meter installed and at a later date wish to change energy supplier, regulations have been put in place to ensure there are no obstacles preventing you from doing so.

If you are planning having Photovoltaic panels installed or any other type of energy generating system, smart meters will calculate whether or not there is a surplus which could be sold back to the Grid.

Under **OFGEN** codes which were published July 2013 it will be down to the consumer how much information your energy supplier can retrieve from your smart meter. Any information you provide to your supplier may only be passed on to a third party with your consent. This allows you to decide whether or not information you provide can be used for marketing purposes.

TELEPHONES

You will need to contact Openreach (BT) before you start any work. They in turn will provide a new site representative to liaise with you and discuss your requirements.

You can contact your new sites office by calling **0800 616 866**.
Your new site representative will be able to advise on the entry points to your new property, either by overhead cabling or by way of an underground duct. If a new telephone line is to be laid underground, Openreach will supply you with all the ducting and draw cables free of charge. You must lay all ducting in accordance with Openreach specifications, including entry points. All this information is available on the Openreach website, which incorporates a developer's step-by-step guide.

MEDIA

There are nowadays many different ways of receiving information into your home: television, broadband or cable are just some of your options. There are also many ways of actually distributing media through the home. With technology moving at a frightening pace it is difficult to predict what additional cabling you may require for the future.

Category 5 cable which is commonly referred to as Cat 5 is used for computer networks. It is reasonably versatile and can be used to carry other signals such as telemetry and video, which makes it an ideal choice for Home Entertainment Systems. With new technologies emerging Cat 5 may no longer be required as there are now numerous wireless systems available on the market.

In conclusion if you are planning installing home entertainment it is best to decide upon your system requirements. If additional cabling is required it will need to be installed at the First Fix stage of your development. There are numerous stores around that specialise in home entertainment and they will advise you what may be required to support the system of your choice. Most suppliers will also carry out the installation of their systems.

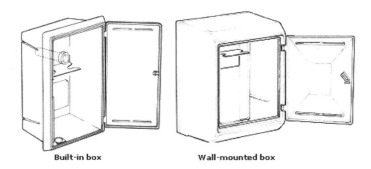

Built-in box   Wall-mounted box

Building regulations now require sound and air testing to take place in certain instances before a Habitation Certificate (sometimes referred to as Completion Certificate) is issued. In both instances the dwelling needs to be complete before any testing can take place.

SOUND TESTING

Sound testing is only necessary if your new dwelling is directly linked to another dwelling; this would usually be a semi-detached or terraced property, or a flat. If your house is detached, sound testing will not be required.

NOISE
ANNOYS

Sound testing has been introduced for new dwellings by way of Building Regulation Approved Document E – Resistance to the passage of sound, its main focus is the separating walls, floors and ceilings from an adjoining property. The document gives advice on methods of construction to enable you to achieve the required levels of sound insulation.

You can either demonstrate the acoustic performance of separating walls, floors and ceilings through pre-completion site testing or by licensing Robust Details.

Robust Details are a set of approved and published design details that can be purchased and registered to a new dwelling. Robust will issue you with a purchase statement which will list the registered dwelling and the relevant detail or details. You will then need to forward a copy of the purchase statement to Building Control before any work commences on site.

Construction must be carried out in accordance with the Robust Details handbook to enable a compliance certificate to be issued.

The compliance certificate shows that you have followed the details and completed their checklist. Building control may wish to see your checklist but apart from that you need do nothing else as far as Part E Robust Details are concerned, avoiding the need for pre completion testing. Robust Details can be found at **www.robustdetails.com**

If you are going down the route of pre-completion site testing you need to ensure that your construction method complies with and passes the required testing procedures.
Listed below are wall treatment methods that are designed to improve airborne sound insulation:

● Render or Parge coat – Parge or render coat is an applied coating to the face of the separating wall before the wall is dry lined or plastered. It will seal any open mortar joints and increase the mass of the wall.

● Construction of an independent wall – You can construct a wall that stands in dependently to an existing separating wall and would normally be constructed of metal stud or timber. The new wall should be separated from the existing wall by 20mm. The studs should then be insulated and boarded with dense plasterboard.

● Cavity fill – Cavity wall insulation will improve airborne sound insulation

12.0
Sound and Air Test

Pre-completion site testing procedures

Testing involves measuring sound insulation of separating walls, floors and ceilings used specialised equipment.

For testing purposes, access will be required to both sides of the separating walls. Carpets should not have been laid. Walls and floors are tested for airborne and impact sound insulation by way of taking a series of readings monitoring background noise levels, reverberation times, airborne and impact testing. Measurements need to be taken from the source room and the receiver room.

Background noise - This is measured in the receiver room so that the sound insulation tests are correct for external sound, such as noise from traffic; the background noise is taken into account when calculating the sound insulation rating for the separating wall.

Reverberation times - These are measured to account for characteristics and absorptiveness of the receiver room. In each room to be tested reverberation time is calculated six times and an average is taken. To measure the reverberation time a speaker is used to generate white noise in such a way to create a diffuse field. The speaker is then instantaneously switched off and a measurement is taken on the length of time it takes for the room to drop by 60dB. This is carried out six times and calculations are applied to determine the insulation performance.

Airborne testing - This is achieved by the use of speakers to generate white noise, usually at levels of 100 decibels, in the source room. Then, using a moving microphone technique, the average sound pressure level is measured. Using the same technique, the average sound pressure level is measured in the receiver room.

Combining the measurements of the airborne test along with reverberation and background time elements, the airborne sound insulation of the separating wall can be calculated.

Sound and Air Test

Impact testing - This is used for testing floors that separate dwellings. In most instances this refers to flats. The impact testing requires a tapping machine which creates sound directly onto the floor construction of the source room; measurements are taken in the receiver room. The impact sound pressure level is calculated giving the floor an impact sound insulation rating. Measurements are taken with the tapping machine in at least four different positions, with at least six measurements taken at each position.

By combining the results of the impact testing with background noise and reverberation time, an impact sound insulation rating can be calculated.

Test Failure

If your dwelling fails its sound test, upgrades or extra sealing will be required to enable you to comply with sound insulation requirements

Airborne sound insulation values must meet minimum values. The higher the figure the more efficient the sound insulation value. Impact testing values must meet the maximum level as the lower the figure the better the performance of the sound insulation.

Approved Document Part E states that new build separating (party) walls must achieve an Airborne sound insulation result of at least 45dB and have an impact sound insulation result of separating floors of different dwellings of no more than 62dB.

It is vital that your sound testing is carried out by an accredited company otherwise building control could refuse to accept the results.

Air Tightness Testing

Air testing for new dwellings forms part of the new dwellings Energy Assessment and the results will be required by Local Authority building control. On a small development where there is to be two or less properties, a test is not mandatory. If you decide not to carry out a test for Energy Assessment purposes a figure of 15m3(h.m2) at 50Pa can be used. This figure is extremely high compared with what can be achieved through good construction practice.

Requirements for air pressure testing are in Building Regulation Approved Document L1A and L2A and set a minimum requirement for testing at a backstop value of 10m3/hr/m2. The actual figure you may require could be significantly lower as it forms part of the SAP calculation. There is often a requirement, where dwellings are built to the sustainable code, that the figures need to be less than 5m3/hr/m2

Dwellings Air tightness is part of the government's ongoing commitment to reduce CO_2 emissions from energy consumption. Good standards for airtightness can be achieved by ensuring all gaps and holes are correctly sealed during the construction process. Air tightness testing is a recognised method of measuring the extent to which air is lost through the building fabric, not through ventilation which is a controlled air flow in and out of a building. Air tightness testing is also referred to as Air leakage test or Air pressure test. Air permeability is quantified as the leakage of air in or out of a dwelling per square metre of the building envelope at a pressure difference of 50Pa (Pascal) between the inside and the outside of a building.

Air testing needs to be carried out as your project nears completion. Ensure all extractor fans and sanitary ware is properly fixed and sealed in place to any open-ended pipe work. Also note that the equipment used for the testing will require a power supply that is live inside the dwelling.

How air pressure tests are carried out:
1- A temporary fan is fitted, usually in an external doorway
2- It is then switched on to extract air from the building
3- Pressure readings are taken and used to measure the amount of air that leaks back into the building per hour
4- The internal area of the floors, roof and walls of the dwelling are then calculated
5- This calculation is then used to find the air permeability in M3 per hour per M2 of building area

Once a property has been tested you will be issued with a report indicating the air permeability. If your desired results are not achieved you will need to locate and prevent excessive air leakage areas of the dwelling and then re-test the dwelling.

Houses are not constructed in a factory environment, they are built in all different weather conditions using materials that will shrink and expand with some materials being irregular in shape. Therefore there are certain permitted tolerances.

The **NHBC (National House Build Council**) have a section in their standards called "A consistent approach to finishes". This section explains the industry acceptable standards for materials and workmanship. If you are intending to consult their standards it must be understood that the tolerances specified are a worst case scenario and a better standard of finish should be aimed for.

Checking to ensure the quality of the labour and materials that go into the construction of your new dwelling is not for the faint-hearted, but there needs to be an ongoing assessment as your project progresses. Some people find it hard to confront contractors and suppliers of materials regarding workmanship and material quality as they expect to get fobbed off with all manner of excuses. If you think this will be the case you need to appoint a person who will do your quality checking for you. You may consider one or more of the following to carry out quality control on your behalf:

- Project Manager
- Surveyor
- Architect
- Clerk of Works

Most good material suppliers and contractors will be happy to change defective materials or rectify any work that is not acceptable, as most of their business is by recommendation and they will not want to get a bad reputation. It is important that all the workmanship and material quality is of an acceptable standard to you. Don't part with any money unless these standards are met.

Section 12P of this book revisits the construction of a dwelling from the start of the project, identifying acceptable standards and items that should be checked during construction. It is important that any workmanship or materials that you find unsatisfactory is rectified immediately, as it could have a knock on effect to the project as a whole.

Listed below is the sequence of checking operations along with items that should be checked. The trades/traders normally responsible for these operations are shown in brackets. Acceptable tolerances have been given where applicable.

Site preparation (Ground Worker)
- Ensure all remediation is complete and certificated if required
- If any demolition is required, everything should be removed from site including old foundations
- All topsoil and any vegetation should be removed from construction area and heaped up for later use
- Access and haul roads should be formed

Foundations (Ground Workers)
- Ensure all foundation designs have been submitted and approved by Local Authority Building Control and your Warranty provider before commencing with foundations
- In the case of strip and trench foundations, ensure the foundation bottom is level, with no soft spots, to a suitable depth and on firm ground
- If any reinforcing or clay board is required ensure it is placed correctly
- Ensure foundations have been inspected before they are poured
- Check the concretes designed mix
- Ensure that the correct amount of concrete has been poured and is left level on top, with any steps formed if necessary

Brickwork to DPC (Bricklayer)
- Ensure the correct mortar is being used (it is generally a different mix below DPC)
- Make sure that you have enough courses of face brickwork showing below DPC, making allowances for finished ground levels.
- All lintels and vents should be correctly positioned
- Once your brickwork is to DPC check all the corners are level. All the corners should be ± 4mm per metre up to 6 metres, but regardless of the total length of the floor should never be more than ± 25mm.

- Face brickwork on plan should not deviate in and out more than ± 8mm in any length of wall up to 5 metres.
- Ensure all bed joints are consistent (bed joints are usually 10mm).

Underground Drainage (Ground Worker)
- Ensure all drainage is laid to the correct falls
- Ensure all runs of drainage are straight
- All pipe bedding should be placed to surround pipes where necessary
- All drainage needs to be inspected before being backfilled
- Ensure suitable backfill material is used
- Make sure all manholes, inspection chambers and rodding access points are all built in the correct positions

Ground Floor Slab (Ground Worker)
- Make sure the sub base is as the design
- Ensure all insulation is correctly placed
- Check that a suitable DPM (Damp Proof Membrane) is in place and jointed correctly where required
- Any required reinforcing should be placed correctly checked
- Make sure that any drainage that comes through the floor is in the correct position
- The floor slab should be inspected by Building Control prior to any concrete being poured
- Check the floors concrete design mix (if applicable)
- The level of the finished floor should be a maximum of 4mm out of level per metre for floors up to 6 metres across, with a maximum of 25mm regardless of the length of the floor
- The flatness of the floor should have a maximum deviation of ± 5mm in any 2 metre length
- Ensure the ground around the outside perimeter of the floor slab is stoned up and level ready for the follow on trades

First Lift Brickwork (Bricklayer)
- Make sure all DPC is placed correctly before any superstructure brickwork is laid
- Check that correct blocks are being used for the inner skin

- Ensure the correct insulation method is being used
- Check that brickwork horizontally does not deviate more than ± 8mm in any length of wall up to 5 metres
- Check that brickwork vertically is a maximum of 8mm out of plumb per 2.5 metres and a maximum total of 12mm for walls over 5 metres
- Check wall ties and wall tie spacings are correct
- Check that all cavities are clean and free of mortar and debris

First lift scaffold (Scaffolder)
- Ensure scaffold is constructed on a firm base
- Make sure all sole plates are in place
- Ensure that the working platform is fit for purpose
- It is the duty of a scaffolder after any adaption has been made to issue you with a handover certificate. Sometimes they will tag the scaffold, which is commonly referred to as a scafftag and will inform the person using it if is safe to use or not.
- Ensure ladders are positioned and secured correctly.
- If loading bays are required ensure they are in place, and with appropriate safety gates fitted.

Brickwork to Joist (Bricklayer)
- Ensure all inner skin block work is built to the correct height ready for the first floor joists to sit on
- Ensure all lintels are positioned correctly, with cavity trays and weep vents where required
- Check dimensions of all window and door openings and that they are positioned correctly
- Make sure all internal block work is to joist height
- Make sure all block work joints are fully filled and flush with the block work
- All brickwork used in superstructure should be of a similar appearance. There may be slight colour differences due to bricks coming from different batches. If different batches are not uniform in colour your brick supplier should be contacted and bricks exchanged if at all possible.
- The mortar mix should also be consistent in colour. Sand used from different quarries can affect mortar colour. Before placing orders for mortar try to get some assurances that the mortar colour match will remain consistent.

First Floor Joists and Decking (Carpenter/Joiner)

- Floor joists should be placed ensuring that the top of the joists are level and flat. All permitted tolerances should be the same as ground floors.
- Check that the floor joists correspond with working drawings to give you a correct storey height. This is crucial as it will affect the staircase.
- Solid floor joist will shrink as the part of the normal drying process; however tolerances should still be met
- Check that any hangers have been correctly fitted and with the correct number of fixings
- Check that an expansion gap of at least 10mm is left around the perimeter of the floor where it meets the internal skin of blockwork
- Check all supporting noggins are in place
- Whatever type of decking is used, make sure that the manufacturer's fixing recommendations have been followed

Brickwork to Wall plate (Bricklayer/Scaffolder/Carpenter/Joiner)

- Ensure all floor joists are built in, making sure there are no open joints
- Check all window reveals ensuring they are plumb and that the deviate to a maximum of 4mm
- Check the scaffold lift before use ensuring a safe and level working platform has been provided and a hand over certificate has been issued
- Check all wall plates are cut with lap joints where necessary and bedded on properly

Roof Construction (Carpenter/Joiner)

- Ensure all wall plate straps are properly fixed at a maximum of 2 metre centres
- Check all roof members are in place in accordance with the design, including all lateral and wind bracing.
- Check that all rafters or trusses are correctly spaced and are plumb.
- Make sure all soffits and fascias are straight, level and have adequate fixings.
- If soffits and fascia boards are timber they should be treated before being fixed.
- Ensure gable ladders and gable restraint straps are in place.

Brickwork Gables (Bricklayer/Scaffolder)

- Ensure the brick and blockwork is neatly cut following the pitch of the roof construction

- Ensure the scaffolder provides tables as safe working platforms for the bricklayers and the roofers; a hand over certificate should be provided.
- Ensure all brickwork is within tolerance.
- Make sure all gable ladders are built in with fully filled joints.

Roof Coverings (Roof Tilers)

- Ensure any ventilation that is required at the eaves is in place before the roof is covered in
- Check that all underlays which may be felt are correct as specified and have been lapped properly
- Ensure that all roof coverings are fixed in accordance with manufacturers recommendations
- Check that all ridge tiles are properly bedded or fixed
- Make sure that all roof covering materials are consistent in size and colour.
- Check all tile vents are fixed in their correct positions
- Check all flashings and any other weathering details are correctly fitted and sealed or pointed as necessary

Guttering and Downspouts (Plumber)

- Ensure all guttering is fixed in place securely with ample supporting brackets and all falling to the outlets is complete
- Downspouts should be fitted vertically, with the roof outlet vertically above the surface water underground drainage outlet, where possible
- Ensure all stop ends have been fitted and leaf guards fitted if required

External Decoration (Decorator)

- Ensure all external decoration is complete including soffits, fascia boards, barge boards and windows. This needs to be done prior to the removal of the scaffolding.

External Render (Plasterer/Scaffolder)

- If your new home is to be rendered, check that all surfaces have been prepared ready to receive the render coat
- Ensure all scaffold is adapted in appropriate lifts to cater for the rendering operation and a scaffold handover certificate is provided
- Excluding features, deviations in render horizontally and vertically should be

to a maximum of ± 8mm in every 5 metres, with a maximum deviation of 4mm in the window reveals.

Removing Scaffold (Scaffolder)

- Prior to removal of the scaffolding take time to check that you are happy with the workmanship and the quality of the materials, especially high level work
- Make sure all materials are removed from the scaffold prior to the scaffolding being dismantled (anything left on a scaffold is likely to get thrown off)
- Ensure all scaffold is removed from site prior to commencement of any external works

First Fix (Carpenter/Joiner)

- Make sure all stairs are fitted securely ensuring all glue blocks and wedges are in place
- Inspect your stairs for damage before they are fitted, making sure you are happy with the quality (stair manufacturers will not take any stairs back once they have been fitted)
- Check that all stud partition walls are plumb and any door openings are of the correct width and in the correct position
- Check all window boards are securely fitted

Windows and External Doors (Window fitter/Carpenter/Joiner)

- Ensure all vertical damp membrane is in place
- Check all windows and doors are installed plumb and not in wind (twisted)
- Ensure sufficient fixings have been used
- Ensure all windows and doors frames are externally sealed
- Check all glazing for scratches. Industry standards recommend that glass should be viewed in daylight from within the room at least 2 metres from the pane looking directly at the glass. If the glazing is laminated, toughened or coated then it should be viewed at a distance of 3 metres.
- Check that all locking mechanisms and hinges operate correctly
- Check that all security features are fitted and lock and un-lock as designed
- Ensure all draft excluders are in place and show no sign of damaged
- Make sure any trickle vents open and close satisfactory

First Fix Plumbing (Plumber)

- Check all pipework is in the correct positions (check against drawings indicating sanitary ware positions and kitchen layouts)
- Ensure all pipe work has been pressure tested prior to plastering (often plumbing contractors will leave pipework on test until plastering is complete. This makes any damage easily identifiable if any pipework gets accidently damaged by screws or nails before the system is second fixed).
- If plastic pipework is to be used ensure the plumber places metal tracer tape around or behind pipe runs. This enables pipe runs to be identified after the walls are plastered.
- Check all gas supply pipes are in the correct positions and can be identified as gas supply

First Fix Electrics (Electrician)

- Make sure all back boxes are securely fixed with at least two screws per box
- Ensure all wiring from the boxes runs vertically or horizontally unless special cable protection has been provided
- Ensure that all heights of switches and sockets comply with Building Regulation Approved Document Part M as indicated below
- Ensure all wiring for alarms, CCTV, media is in place.

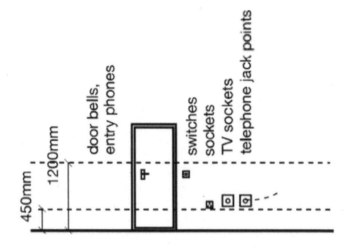

Plastering and Dry Lining (Plasterers)

- Do not proceed with any plastering or boarding until it has been inspected by local building control and your warranty provider
- Ensure all required insulation is in place prior to boarding
- Check correct boards are being used in the correct positions, such as sound block and fire resistance
- Make sure all correct fixings are being used to secure boards
- Where Dot and Dab is used to fix boards ensure there are solid dabs around sockets and switches and along the bottom of each board to enable skirting boards to be securely fixed
- Wall and ceiling surfaces should have a maximum deviation of ± 5mm per 2 metres
- Walls should be no more than 8mm out of plumb per storey height
- Window reveals should be no more than 10mm out of square, unless designed in such a way, such as splayed reveals
- As plaster dries it will shrink, cracking on walls up to 2mm is acceptable and 4mm where plasterwork meets the string of staircases

Second Fix Joinery (Carpenter/Joiner)

- Ensure all skirting and architraves have tight mitre joints
- Make sure all handrails and balustrades are securely fixed in place and at the correct heights, with maximum gaps between spindles not exceeding 100mm
- Ensure all doors have a consistent gap between the door edge and the frame when in the closed position. This should be about 5mm although no industry standard is given.
- Ensure all hinges are fixed allowing doors to open and close freely and that are there no screws missing
- Check that all door handles and locks operate correctly and when doors are closed they do not rattle
- Check that all pipe boxings are neatly fixed

Kitchens (Kitchen Fitter)

- Ensure all base and kitchen units are fixed securely back to the walls
- Ensure all units are level and plumb
- Ensure all worktops have been fixed securely with any joints tight and neat

Checking and Ensuring Quality

- Check all doors and drawers are in line and all gaps are consistent
- Ensure all handles are fitted
- Check all units and doors for damage
- Closely inspect worktops for damage and scratches from a recommended distance of 0.5 metres in daylight or fixed lighting
- Check all drawers and doors open and close smoothly
- Check all plinths are in place
- Ensure all edging strips have been put on
- Check all shelving is in place and has been fitted horizontally
- Ensure the kitchen fitter removes all packaging and debris associated with fitting the kitchen from site on completion

Wall and Floor Tiling (Tiler)
- Ensure all tiles are consistent in colour and texture when purchased
- Ensure all floors and walls are flat and have been correctly prepared prior to any tiling
- All tile joints should be in alignment unless the tiles are designed to be fixed in irregular patterns
- Floor tile joints should be a minimum of 3mm to allow for expansion unless otherwise specified by the manufacturer
- Wall tile joints should be a minimum of 1mm to allow for expansion
- If tiles are to be laid on timber floors ensure flexible adhesives and grouts are used
- Wall and floor tiles should not exceed a deviation of ± 3mm per 2 metres
- Ensure all surplus grout is removed from the tiled areas
- Tiling should have a uniform appearance, with any vertical cuts being equal at each end of the same wall
- When tiling in wet rooms ensure the appropriate adhesive and grout is used

Second Fix Plumbing (Plumber)
- Ensure all radiators have secure fixings and are level and free from damage when fixed
- Check all sanitary ware for signs of damage and scratches
- Make sure all shower doors operate freely and do not leak
- Check all pipe work that is not to be covered is fixed neatly

- Ensure that hot taps are always fitted on the left (this is for the benefit of partially-sighted people)
- Check all sink, basin and kitchen wastes for signs of leaks
- Ensure the heating system runs smoothly and quietly, making sure all excess air has been purged from the system
- Check all soil vent pipes have been correctly fixed and extended through the roof where required
- Check all toilets flush correctly
- Check all bath, shower and toilet seats are all fitted correctly and match the sanitary ware in design and colour
- Check all gas fires and gas hobs are connected

Second fix Electrics (Electrician)

- Check all switches and sockets are fitted level and securely back to the wall.
- Check all extractor fans are fitted and working
- Check that all light switches work correctly especially where there is dual switching for the same light
- Ensure all appliances are wired and working correctly
- Make sure all earth bonding is done, including gas supply
- Ensure the correct amounts of low energy light fittings have been fixed
- Check all smoke detectors are working
- Check carbon monoxide monitors are fitted and working
- Check any door bells are working

Decoration (Painter and Decorator)

- Check all external woodwork has been primed, undercoated and top coated, and any other desired finishes, such as varnish, have been applied to a good standard
- Check all walls and ceilings have been properly prepared prior to the top coat of emulsion
- Check all woodwork has been filled, rubbed down and caulked before the final finish has been applied
- Check the finish of all woodwork for runs and make sure the finish is reasonably smooth
- Check that any areas where intumescent paint is required has been carried out in accordance with design specifications

Cleaning (Cleaner)

You may wish to carry out the cleaning yourself; however there are companies that specialise in new build cleans. If you employ one of these companies, before you sign off their work, check the following points have been done to a satisfactory standard:

- All protective films are removed from sanitary ware, kitchens and windows
- All floors are cleaned removing and mortar or plaster
- All kitchen cupboards are cleaned out
- Paint splashes are removed from sockets, light switches and window frames.
- All glazing inside and out is cleaned
- Check all sanitary ware is cleaned
- All wall tiling is cleaned and polished, removing any excess grout
- All window and door frames are cleaned, both internally and externally
- All rubbish is removed from the property

Sealant (Sealant Application Contractor)

- Ensure all sealant has a neat and smooth surface finish
- Check the correct sealants have been used, such as frame sealants and sanitary ware sealants
- Check intumescent sealant has been applied to the perimeter of integral garage ceiling if applicable

External Works (Groundworkers/Fencers/Landscapers/Bricklayers)

- Allowances should be made for settlement; any movement should only be minor
- Ensure all drain covers are level with adjacent finished ground levels
- Check that drives and paths have no standing water after rainfall. The permissible standard is one hour after rainfall has stopped, any areas of standing water should be no deeper than 5mm (as a rough guide it should not cover a one pound coin) or exceed 1m2. Any standing water is not permitted adjacent to any entrance or exit doors.
- Deviations in surface finishes, such as drives and paths, should not exceed ± 10mm from a 2 metre straight edge
- Ensure top soil is of a suitable depth; a recommended minimum is 100mm but ideally it should be at least 150mm

Checking and Ensuring Quality

- Ensure correct boundary positions have been established before you erect any fence or boundary walls. This can normally be checked against Deed plans.
- Ensure all rainwater downspouts are directed into the surface water drainage system
- Ensure all fencing is secure and gates are fitted with suitable latches and bolts
- Ensure all required visibility splays are in place before any occupation has taken place (this may require removal of hedges or fencing)

Garages (General)
- Ensure all garage doors are properly fitted and can be secured
- For integral garages ensure any personal doors are fitted with closers and intumescent fire seals
- Ensure garage floor slabs slope towards the front of the garage
- Due to thermal shrinkage blockwork in garages may crack; cracking up to 2mm is deemed acceptable
- Ensure all gutters and downspouts have been fitted

There will be many different construction methods used in varying projects and quality checking may need to be tailored to your own project, but it is important to check and question any contractors working on your project.

It is sad to say but true of some contractors, that if they think they can get away with cutting corners they will.

It is common for customers to retain part of the contract fee over an agreed maintenance period to ensure that any remedial work that may be required is carried out. This could be a period of 6 to 12 months; retentions are usually around 5% or an agreed amount. If retention is to be held it will need to be negotiated at the tendering stage.

Note
If it doesn't look right, it probably isn't

BUILD YOUR OWN
HOUSE

During the planning process and the construction phase you will be issued with a number of certificates all of which require collating and will have to be used as evidence when obtaining an Occupation Certificate and your Structural Warranty.

This section sets out the certificates you will need and who will require copies. Examples of the certificates have been included in the section.

Occupation Certificate
(sometimes referred to as a Habitation Certificate)

Address   Certificate No.

BC 67

Dated

 BOROUGH OF BARROW-IN-FURNESS

LABC OCCUPATION CERTIFICATE

BOROUGH OF **BARROW IN FURNESS**

I certify that, in my opinion, the property now known as   (Address) **Barrow-in-Furness Cumbria** is fit for occupation. Such inspections as have been made have not revealed any failure to comply with Building Regulations or significant departures from the plans register No. FV/2009/0121/ 1 approved by the Borough Council on 19/03/2009.

Building Control
Town Hall,
Duke Street,
Barrow-in-Furness,
Cumbria, LA14 2LD   PRINCIPAL BUILDING CONTROL SURVEYOR

Occupation Certificates are issued by Local Authority building control. For this certificate to be issued they will have satisfactorily carried out all inspections during the construction process, including a final inspection. They will also require the following certification:

An EPC (Energy Performance Certificate) along with SAP (Standard Assessment Procedure) calculations

BUILD YOUR OWN
HOUSE

Energy Performance Certificate

S A P

ADDRESS	Dwelling type: Detached house
	Date of assessment: 05 February 2012
	Date of certificate: 07 February 2012
	Reference number:
	Type of assessment: SAP, new dwelling
	Total floor area: 190.59 m²

This home's performance is rated in terms of the energy use per square metre of floor area, energy efficiency based on fuel costs and environmental impact based on carbon dioxide (CO_2) emissions.

Energy Efficiency Rating

	Current	Potential

Very energy efficient - lower running costs

(92 plus) A
(81-91) B
(69-80) C
(55-68) D
(39-54) E
(21-38) F
(1-20) G

80   81

Not energy efficient - higher running costs

England & Wales   EU Directive 2002/91/EC

The energy efficiency rating is a measure of the overall efficiency of a home. The higher the rating the more energy efficient the home is and the lower the fuel bills are likely to be.

Environmental Impact (CO_2) Rating

	Current	Potential

Very environmentally friendly - lower CO_2 emissions

(92 plus) A
(81-91) B
(69-80) C
(55-68) D
(39-54) E
(21-38) F
(1-20) G

79   80

Not environmentally friendly - higher CO_2 emissions

England & Wales   EU Directive 2002/91/EC

The environmental impact rating is a measure of a home's impact on the environment in terms of carbon dioxide (CO_2) emissions. The higher the rating the less impact it has on the environment.

Estimated energy use, carbon dioxide (CO_2) emissions and fuel costs of this home

	Current	Potential
Energy use	100 kWh/m²per year	95 kWh/m²per year
Carbon dioxide emissions	3.6 tonnes per year	3.5 tonnes per year
Lighting	£133 per year	£84 per year
Heating	£554 per year	£561 per year
Hot water	£101 per year	£101 per year

The figures in the table above have been provided to enable prospective buyers and tenants to compare the fuel costs and carbon emissions of one home with another. To enable this comparison the figures have been calculated using standardised running conditions (heating periods, room temperatures, etc.) that are the same for all homes, consequently they are unlikely to match an occupier's actual fuel bills and carbon emissions in practice. The figures do not include the impacts of the fuels used for cooking or running appliances, such as TV, fridge etc.; nor do they reflect the costs associated with service, maintenance or safety inspections. Always check the certificate date because fuel prices can change over time and energy saving recommendations will evolve.

recommended

Remember to look for the Energy Saving Trust Recommended logo when buying energy-efficient products. It's a quick and easy way to identify the most energy-efficient products on the market.

For advice on how to take action and to find out about offers available to help make your home more energy efficient, call 0800 512 012 or visit www.energysavingtrust.org.uk

BUILD YOUR OWN
HOUSE

About this document

The Energy Performance Certificate for this dwelling was produced following an energy assessment undertaken by a qualified assessor, accredited by Elmhurst Energy Systems Ltd, to a scheme authorised by the Government. This certificate was produced using the SAP 2009 assessment methodology and has been produced under the Energy Performance of Buildings (Certificates and Inspections) (England and Wales) Regulations 2007 as amended. A copy of the certificate has been lodged on a national register.

Assessor's accreditation number:
Assessor's name:
Company name/trading name:
Address:
Phone number:
Fax number:
E-mail address:
Related party disclosure:

If you have a complaint or wish to confirm that the certificate is genuine

Details of the assessor and the relevant accreditation scheme are as above. You can get contact details of the accreditation scheme from their website at www.elmhurstenergy.co.uk together with details of their procedures for confirming authenticity of a certificate and for making a complaint.

About the building's performance ratings

The ratings on the certificate provide a measure of the building's overall energy efficiency and its environmental impact, calculated in accordance with a national methodology that takes into account factors such as insulation, heating and hot water systems, ventilation and fuels used. The average Energy Efficiency Rating for a dwelling in England and Wales is band E (rating 50).

Not all buildings are used in the same way, so energy ratings use 'standard occupancy' assumptions which may be different from the specific way you use your home. Different methods of calculation are used for homes and for other buildings. Details can be found at www.communities.gov.uk/epbd.

Buildings that are more energy efficient use less energy, save money and help protect the environment. A building with a rating of 100 would cost almost nothing to heat and light and would cause almost no carbon emissions. The potential ratings on the certificate describe how close this building could get to 100 if all the cost effective recommended improvements were implemented.

About the impact of buildings on the environment

One of the biggest contributors to global warming is carbon dioxide. The way we use energy in buildings causes emissions of carbon. The energy we use for heating, lighting and power in homes produces over a quarter of the UK's carbon dioxide emissions and other buildings produce a further one-sixth.

The average household causes about 6 tonnes of carbon dioxide every year. Adopting the recommendations in this report can reduce emissions and protect the environment. You could reduce emissions even more by switching to renewable energy sources. In addition there are many simple everyday measures that will save money, improve comfort and reduce the impact on the environment. Some examples are given at the end of this report.

**Visit the Department for Communities and Local Government website at
www.communities.gov.uk/epbd to:**

- Find how to confirm the authenticity of an energy performance certificate
- Find how to make a complaint about a certificate or the assessor who produced it
- Learn more about the national register where this certificate has been lodged - the Department is the controller of the data on the register for Data Protection Act 1998 purposes
- Learn more about energy efficiency and reducing energy consumption

BUILD YOUR OWN
HOUSE

Address :
07 February 2012 RRN:

Recommendations

Recommendations

The measures below are cost effective. The performance ratings after improvement listed below are cumulative, that is they assume the improvements have been installed in the order that they appear in the table. The indicative costs are representative for most properties but may not apply in a particular case.

Lower cost measures	Indicative Cost	Typical savings per year	Ratings after improvement	
			Energy Efficiency	Environmental Impact
1 Low energy lighting for all fixed outlets	£28	£42	B 81	C 80
Total		£42		

Further measures to achieve even higher standards

The further measures listed below should be considered in addition to those already specified if aiming for the highest possible standards for this home. However you should check the conditions in any covenants, planning conditions, warranties or sale contracts. The indicative costs are representative for most properties but may not apply in a particular case.

2 Solar photovoltaic panels, 2.5 kWp	£11,000 - £20,000	£227	B 87	B 85

Enhanced energy efficiency rating	B 87
Enhanced environmental impact (CO_2) rating	B 85

Improvements to the energy efficiency and environmental impact ratings will usually be in step with each other. However, they can sometimes diverge because reduced energy costs are not always accompanied by a reduction in carbon dioxide (CO_2) emissions.

Address:
07 February 2012 RRN:

Energy Report

Summary of this home's energy performance related features

The following is an assessment of the key individual elements that have an impact on this home's performance rating. Each element is assessed by the national calculation methodology; 1 star means least efficient and 5 stars means most efficient

Element	Description	Current performance	
		Energy Efficiency	Environmental
Walls	Average thermal transmittance 0.29 W/m²	★ ★ ★ ★ ★	★ ★ ★ ★ ★
Roof	Average thermal transmittance 0.14 W/m²	★ ★ ★ ★ ★	★ ★ ★ ★ ★
Floor	Average thermal transmittance 0.21 W/m²	★ ★ ★ ★	★ ★ ★ ★
Windows	High performance glazing	★ ★ ★ ★ ★	★ ★ ★ ★ ★
Main heating	Boiler and underfloor heating, mains gas	★ ★ ★ ★	★ ★ ★ ★
Main heating controls	Time and temperature zone control	★ ★ ★ ★ ★	★ ★ ★ ★ ★
Secondary heating	None	—	—
Hot water	From main system	★ ★ ★ ★	★ ★ ★ ★
Lighting	Low energy lighting in 42% of fixed outlets	★ ★ ★	★ ★ ★
Air Tightness	Air permeability 9.3 m³/h.m²(as tested)	★ ★ ★	★ ★ ★

Current energy efficiency rating	C 80
Current environmental impact (CO_2) rating	C 79

Thermal transmittance is a measure of the rate of heat loss through a building element; the lower the value the better the energy performance.
Air permeability is a measure of the air tightness of a building; the lower the value the better the air tightness.

Low and zero carbon energy sources

None

BUILD YOUR OWN
HOUSE

Address: Recommendations
07 February 2012 RRN:

About the cost effective measures to improve this home's performance ratings

Lower cost measures

These measures are relatively inexpensive to install and are worth tackling first. The indicative costs of measures included earlier in this EPC include the costs of professional installation in most cases. Some of the cost effective measures below may be installed as DIY projects which will reduce the cost. DIY is not always straightforward, and sometimes there are health and safety risks, so take advice before carrying out DIY improvements.

1 Low energy lighting

Replacement of traditional light bulbs with energy saving recommended ones will reduce lighting costs over the lifetime of the bulb, and they last up to 12 times longer than ordinary light bulbs. Also consider selecting low energy light fittings when redecorating; contact the Lighting Association for your nearest stockist of Domestic Energy Efficient Lighting Scheme fittings.

About the further measures to achieve even higher standards

Further measures that could deliver even higher standards for this home. You should check the conditions in any covenants, planning conditions, warranties or sale contracts before undertaking any of these measures. If you are a tenant, before undertaking any work you should check the terms of your lease and obtain approal from your landlord if the lease either requires it, or makes no express provision for such work.

2 Solar photovoltaic (PV) panels

A solar PV system is one which converts light directly into electricity via panels placed on the roof with no waste and no emissions. This electricity is used throughout the home in the same way as the electricity purchased from an energy supplier. The British Photovoltaic Association has up-to-date information on local installers who are qualified electricians and on any grant that may be available. Planning restrictions may apply in certain neighbourhoods and you should check this with the local authority. Building Regulations apply to this work, so your local authority building control department should be informed, unless the installer is appropriately qualified and registered as such with a competent persons scheme[1], and can therefore self-certify the work for Building Regulation compliance. The assessment does not include the effect of any feed-in tariff, which could appreciably increase the savings that are shown on this EPC for solar photovoltaic panels.

What can I do today?

Actions that will save money and reduce the impact of your home on the environment include:

- Ensure that you understand the dwelling and how its energy systems are intended to work so as to obtain the maximum benefit in terms of reducing energy use and CO_2emissions. The papers you are given by the builder and the warranty provider will help you in this.
- Check that your heating system thermostat is not set too high (in a home, 21°C in the living room is suggested) and use the timer to ensure you only heat the building when necessary.
- Make sure your hot water is not too hot - a cylinder thermostat need not normally be higher than 60°C
- Turn off lights when not needed and do not leave appliances on standby. Remember not to leave chargers (e.g. for mobile phones) turned on when you are not using them.
- Close your curtains at night to reduce heat escaping through the windows.
- If you're not filling up the washing machine, tumble dryer or dishwasher, use the half-load or economy programme.

Building Regulation Compliance		Page 1 of 3

Users Ref:

Property:

Issued on: 7.February.2012

Prop Type Ref:

DER: 20.52

TER: 20.79

SAP Rating:	80 C	**SAP Energy Cost:** £409.37	**CO2 Emissions:** 3.68 t/year
EI Rating:	79 C	**Energy used:** 117 kWh/m2/year	**Enel:** 0 **ZC:** 0.00

Surveyor:
Address:
Client:

Software Version: EES SAP 2005.018.03, October 2009 (Design System), BRE SAP Worksheet 9.81

SAP version: 9.81 Regs Region: England and Wales (Part L1A 2006), Calculation Type: New Build

CHECKLIST FOR DWELLING AS BUILT

Site reference		Plot reference		
Builder		Contact		Tel:
Builder Control body		Contact		Tel:
SAP assessment by		Contact		Tel:

Evidence of competency:

No.	Check	Evidence	Produced by	Design OK
1	**Criterion 1: Predicted carbon dioxide emission from proposed dwelling does not exceed the target.**			
1.1	**TER** (kg CO_2/m^2)	*Main fuel - Gas* *Fuel factor = 1.00* *TER = 20.79*	Authorised SAP Assessor	N/A
1.2	**DER** for dwelling as built (kg CO_2/m^2)	*DER = 20.52*	Authorised SAP Assessor	N/A
1.3	Are emissions from dwelling as built less than or equal to the target?	*DER 20.52 < TER 20.79*	Authorised SAP Assessor	OK
2	**Criterion 2: The performance of the building fabric and the heating, hot water and fixed lighting systems should be no worse than the design limits.**			
2.1	**Fabric U-values** Are all U-values better than the design limits in Table 2?	*Element Average Highest* *Wall 0.29 (0.35) 0.30 (0.70) OK* *Roof 0.14 (0.25) 0.14 (0.35) OK* *Floor 0.21 (0.25) 0.26 (0.70) OK* *Openings 1.72 (2.20) 3.00 (3.30) OK*	Authorised SAP Assessor	OK
	Common areas in buildings with multiple dwellings (where relevant)			
2.2	If the common areas are un-heated, are all U-values better than the limits in Table 2? (If heated, use L-2A)	Schedule of U-values	Builder's submission	N/A
	Heating and hot water systems			
2.3	Does the efficiency of the heating systems meet the minimum value set out in the Domestic Heating	*Main heating system:* *Post 98 Gas condens. (incl combis)* *with auto ign. F.A.F., Pumped: pump in heated space* *Efficiency - Database: 91.2%* *Minimum permitted: 86.0% - OK* *Secondary heating: None*	Authorised SAP Assessor	OK
2.4	Does the insulation of the hot water cylinder meet the standards set out in the Domestic Heating	*Cylinder:* *Volume = 250 litres* *Nominal cylinder loss: 2.22 kWh/day* *Permitted by DHCG: 3.56 kWh/day - OK* *Primary pipework insulated: Yes - OK*	Authorised SAP Assessor	OK

Building Regulation Compliance			Page 2 of 3

Users Ref: **Issued on:** 7.February.2012

Prop Type Ref:

Property: **DER:** 20.52

                                 TER: 20.79

SAP Rating: 80 C	**SAP Energy Cost:** £409.37	**CO2 Emissions:** 3.68 t/year
EI Rating: 79 C	**Energy used:** 117 kWh/m2/year	**Enel:** 0 **ZC:** 0.00

Surveyor:
Address:
Client:

Software Version: EES SAP 2005.018.03, October 2009 (Design System), BRE SAP Worksheet 9.81
SAP version: 9.81 Regs Region: England and Wales (Part I.1A 2006), Calculation Type: New Build

CHECKLIST FOR DWELLING AS BUILT

No.	Check	Evidence	Produced by	Design OK
2.5	Do controls meet the minimum controls provision set out in the Domestic Heating Compliance	Space heating control: *Time and temperature zone control - OK* Hot water control: *Cylinder thermostat - OK* *Separate water control - OK*	Authorised SAP Assessor	OK
2.6	Does the heating and hot water system meet the other minimum provisions in the Domestic Heating	Schedule of compliance provisions	Builder's submission	
	Fixed internal and external lighting			
2.7	Does fixed internal lighting comply with paragraphs 42 and 44?	Schedule of installed fixed internal lighting *Light fittings: 19, L.E.L. fittings: 8 = 42.00% > 25% - OK* *L.E.L. fittings required per 25m2 or part of TFA: 8 = 8 - OK*	Builder's submission (see schedule below)	OK
2.8	Does the external lighting comply with paragraph 45?	Schedule of installed external lighting *External lights: None*	Builder's submission (see schedule below)	OK
3	**Criterion 3: The dwelling has appropriate passive control measures to limit solar gains.**			
3.1	Does the dwelling have a strong tendency to high summertime temperatures?	*Region: North West England (14)* *Thermal mass parameter = 8.0* *Ventilation rate in hot weather = 4.0* *Overheating risk (Orientation 'SE') = Not significant - OK*	Authorised SAP Assessor	OK
4	**Criterion 4: The performance of the dwelling, as built, is consistent with the DER.**			
4.1	Have the key features of the design been included (or bettered) in practice?	*Wall U-value 0.22 < 0.28* *Roof U-value 0.14 < 0.15* *Boiler efficiency 91.2% (> 90.0%)* *Openings U-value 1.60 < 1.80* *Openings U-value 1.70 < 1.80* *Openings U-value 1.40 < 1.80*	Authorised SAP Assessor	N/A
	Fabric construction			
4.2	Have accredited details been adopted?	Schedule of details used and their reference codes.	Builder's submission	
4.3	Have non-accredited details been used?	Evidence that details conform to standards set out in IP/06.	Builder's submission	
4.4	Has satisfactory documentary evidence of site inspection checks been produced?	Completed pro-formas showing checklists have been completed.	Builder's submission	N/A
4.5	**Actual air permeability** $(m^3/(h.m^2 \text{ at } 50Pa))$	*Actual air permeability = 9.3*	Authorised SAP Assessor	OK

Collating Certification & Commissioning

Building Regulation Compliance	Page 3 of 3

Users Ref:

Issued on: 7.February.2012

Prop Type Ref:

Property:

DER: 20.52

TER: 20.79

SAP Rating:	80 C	SAP Energy Cost: £409.37	CO2 Emissions: 3.68 t/year
EI Rating:	79 C	Energy used: 117 kWh/m2/year	Ene1: 0 ZC: 0.00

Surveyor:

Address:

Client:

Software Version: EES SAP 2005.018.03, October 2009 (Design System), BRE SAP Worksheet 9.81

SAP version: 9.81 Regs Region: England and Wales (Part L1A 2006), Calculation Type: New Build

CHECKLIST FOR DWELLING AS BUILT

No.	Check	Evidence	Produced by	Design OK
4.6	Has evidence been provided that demonstrates that the **Actual air permeability** has been achieved	Sample pressure test results in comparison to design value.	Builder's submission (see schedule below)	N/A
	Commissioning heating and hot water systems			
4.7	Evidence that the heating and hot water systems have been commissioned satisfactorily	Commissioning completion certificate	Builder's submission (see schedule below)	N/A
5	Criterion 5: The necessary provisions for energy efficient operation of the dwelling are put in place.			
5.1	Has all the relevant information been provided?	O&M instructions *SAP = 80*	Builder's submission	N/A

Schedule of supporting competencies

No.	Organisation providing evidence	Telephone	Evidence of competency
2.7			
2.8			
4.6			
4.7			

If you are not building to Code for Sustainable Homes but are conforming to Building Regulation Approved Document Part L (this will depend on the date of your planning approval) you will need to obtain a Nil-Rated Certificate.

If you are building to a Code for Sustainable Homes you will need to produce a Final Certificate. Code is managed by BRE Global Ltd and they are under contract to Communities and Local Government. To gain a Certificate you will need to be assessed by a Code Service provider. Local authority will require a design-stage assessment and a post-construction assessment.

Nil-Rated Certificate

THE CODE FOR SUSTAINABLE HOMES

This Home

Address
Address

This home is designed to meet the requirements of current building regulations.

It is not assessed against the Code for Sustainable Homes. The Code sets higher standards for a range of environmental sustainability features than current Building Regulations. It covers issues such as energy/carbon dioxide emissions, water efficiency and the use of materials.

As this home is not assessed against the Code for Sustainable Homes it can not be certified to meet the enhanced environmental performance standards set out in the Code.

The energy performance of this home will be shown on the Energy Performance Certificate.

NIL RATED

---   ---
Developer   Date

Rating system:
Nil rating: A home that has not been designed and built to meet the standards set out in the Code for Sustainable Homes. It has therefore not been formally assessed against the Code and has a 'Nil rating'
1-6 star rating: A home that has been designed and built to the sustainability standards set out in the Code for Sustainable Homes. A 1 star home is entry level and a 6 star home being a highly sustainable, zero carbon home.

More information can be found at www.communities.gov.uk/thecode

Example Code Certificate

THE CODE FOR SUSTAINABLE HOMES

FINAL CERTIFICATE
(Issued at the Post Construction Stage)

ISSUED TO:
Test House, 1 Test Street,
Test Town, Test Country
TE1 ST1

The sustainability of this home has been independently assessed at the Post Construction Stage and has achieved a Code rating of 5 out of 6 stars under the April 2007 version.

Above Regulatory Standards	Current Best Practice	Highly Sustainable and Zero Carbon

The next page sets out how this home achieved its rating in the nine categories.

Licensed Assessor	Assessor Organisation
Mr L Assessor	**The Assessors**

Client	Developer
C L Ient Ltd	**D E Veloper Inc**

Architect	Certificate Number
Arc I Tects	**TEST – Certificate No 1**

Date	Signed for and on behalf of BRE Global Ltd
12 Never 2008	

This certificate remains the property of [Code Service Provider] and is issued subject to terms and conditions. Copies can be made for the purposes of the Home Information Packs. It is produced from data supplied by the licensed Code assessor. To check the authenticity of this certificate please contact BRE Global Ltd.

Code Service Provider logo

BUILD YOUR OWN
HOUSE

THE CODE FOR SUSTAINABLE HOMES

THE CODE FOR
SUSTAINABLE
HOMES™

FINAL CERTIFICATE
(Issued at the Post Construction Stage)

Certificate Number: TEST – Certificate No 1   **Score: 150**

What Your Code Star Rating Means

Combined Score	36-47	48-56	57-67	68-83	84-89	90-100
Stars	1	2	3	4	5	6

The Code for Sustainable Homes considers the effects on the environment caused by the development and occupation of a home. To achieve a star rating a home must perform better than a new home built to minimum legal standards, and much better than an average existing home.

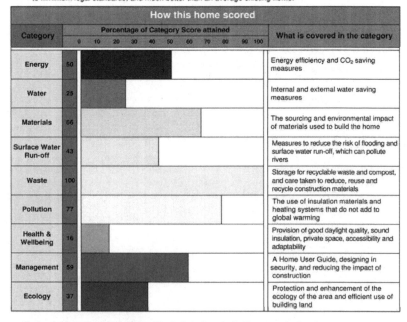

How this home scored		
Category	Percentage of Category Score attained	What is covered in the category
Energy	50	Energy efficiency and CO_2 saving measures
Water	25	Internal and external water saving measures
Materials	66	The sourcing and environmental impact of materials used to build the home
Surface Water Run-off	43	Measures to reduce the risk of flooding and surface water run-off, which can pollute rivers
Waste	100	Storage for recyclable waste and compost, and care taken to reduce, reuse and recycle construction materials
Pollution	77	The use of insulation materials and heating systems that do not add to global warming
Health & Wellbeing	16	Provision of good daylight quality, sound insulation, private space, accessibility and adaptability
Management	59	A Home User Guide, designing in security, and reducing the impact of construction
Ecology	37	Protection and enhancement of the ecology of the area and efficient use of building land

Further detailed information regarding The Code for Sustainable Homes can be found at
www.communities.gov.uk/thecode

Communities
and Local Government

Code Service
Provider logo

You will need to produce the following certification showing that your dwelling is compliant with the following:

- Air Tightness Test Certificate
- Acoustic Test Certificate
- Gas Safe Certificate
- Electrical Installation Certificate

Energy assessments and certification

Our ref: 7th February 2012

Air Permeability Test Report
(ADDRESS)

Test result: 9.31 m³/h.m² (Pass)

Site Address: New detached dwelling

Client:

Tester:

SUMMARY OF AIR PERMIABILITY TEST

In accordance with Approved Document L1A, an air permeability test has been carried out by   (COMPANY)   at the following new dwelling:

(ADDRESS)

The test was performed by a tester approved by The British Institute of Non-Destructive Testing following the procedure given in Technical Standard 1 of the Air Tightness Testing and Measurement Association (ATTMA).

In order to pass the test the Measured Air Permeability is required to be no greater than the Design Air Permeability value assumed in the SAP assessment carried out for the dwelling. Information regarding SAP assessment was provided prior to performing the test.

A summary of the test is given in the table below:

Date	Plot	Plot type	Design Air Permeability (m³/(h.m²) at 50Pa)	Measured Air Permeability (m³/(h.m²) at 50Pa)	Pass / Fail
07.02.12	37	**Detached house**	10.00	9.31	**Pass**

The following appendixes contain supporting information as described:

Appendix A: BINDT air permeability test certificate

Appendix B: Air permeability test report

Appendix C: Register of equipment

Air Permeability Test Certificate

Test number .... BINDT registration number ....

Report reference number ....

This is to certify that the following dwelling and test results were carried out fully in compliance with Approved Document L1 of the 2010 Building Regulations

Dwelling plot/address

House/plot number and road name ....

Town ....

County ....

Country ...UK...............

Post Code ....

Unit type ...Detached house...............

Test date ...7th Feb 2012............ Test time ...12:25...............

Design air permeability	10.00 m³/(h.m²)	$r^2 =$ 0.99786 (>0.98)
Measured air permeability	9.31 m³/(h.m²)	$n =$ 0.603 (1≥n≥0.5)
Envelope area of dwelling	452.98 m²	

Accredited tester

Name .... Signature .... Organisation ....

Telephone number .... e-mail ....

Carried out for .... (Developer/owner/other)

Town ....

County ....

Country ...UK...............

Company stamp

This certificate is issued in compliance with the Competent Persons' Scheme administered by the British Institute of Non-Destructive Testing on behalf of the Secretary of State for the Department for Communities and Local Government.

BUILDING LEAKAGE TEST

Date of Test: 07.02.12   Technician:
Test File:

Customer: Building Address: Detached house

Test Results at 50 Pascals:
  V50: Airflow (m³/h)   4215 (+/- 0.5 %)
  n50: Air Changes per Hour (1/h)
  w50:
  q50: m³/(h*m²) Surface Area   9.31

Leakage Areas: 1782.8 cm² (+/- 2.4 %) Canadian EqLA @ 10 Pa or 3.94 cm²/m² Surface Area
                                 989.8 cm² (+/- 3.9 %) LBL ELA @ 4 Pa or 2.19 cm²/m² Surface Area

Building Leakage Curve: Air Flow Coefficient (Cenv) = 386.5 (+/- 6.1 %)
                                 Air Leakage Coefficient (CL) = 398.6 (+/- 6.1 %)
                                 Exponent (n) = 0.603 (+/- 0.016)
                                 Correlation Coefficient = 0.99786

Test Standard: EN 13829   Test Mode: Depressurization
Type of Test Method: B   Regulation complied with: Approved Document L1A
Equipment: Model 3 Minneapolis Blower Door, S/N 12737

Inside Temperature: 20 ℃   Volume:
Outside Temperature: 4 ℃   Surface Area: 453 m²
Barometric Pressure: 103690 Pa   Floor Area:
Wind Class: 0 Calm   Uncertainty of
Building Wind Exposure: Highly Protected Building   Building Dimensions: 2 %
Type of Heating: Gas central heating with radi.Year of Construction: 2012
Type of Air Conditioning: None
Type of Ventilation: Natural ventilation

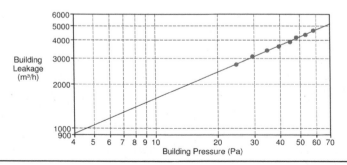

Collating Certification & Commissioning

BUILDING LEAKAGE TEST   Page 2

Date of Test: 07.02.12   Test File:

Comments

Items sealed: extracts to cooker hood, utility, WC, bathroom, en-suites 1 2.
Trickle vents sealed.
Construction and decorations complete.

Data Points: Depressurization

Nominal Building Pressure (Pa)	Fan Pressure (Pa)	Nominal Flow (m³/h)	Temperature Adjusted Flow (m³/h)	% Error	Fan Configuration
-1.4	n/a				
-60.1	38.3	4812	4647	0.6	Open
-55.3	33.5	4513	4358	-0.7	Open
-50.1	30.6	4325	4176	1.3	Open
-46.8	26.3	4023	3885	-1.6	Open
-41.4	155.7	3753	3624	-0.9	Ring A
-36.5	136.9	3527	3406	0.8	Ring A
-31.3	112.3	3207	3096	1.1	Ring A
-26.4	86.2	2822	2724	-0.7	Ring A
-2.4	n/a				

Test 1   Baseline (Pa):   p01- = -1.4   p01+ = 0.0   p02- = -2.4   p02+ = 0.0

An Electrical installation certificate will be issued to you by your electrician.
Your electrical contractor will need to be registered with a recognised body,
such as **NICEIC or NAPIT**

An acoustic test certificate will only be required if your new dwelling is connected to a neighbouring property by a separating wall or floor. If it is and you have registered and built to Robust Details a certificate will not be required.

DETAILS COMPLIANCE CERTIFICATE

Plot Address

Plot 2
Saxon Lane
Off Draper Road
Luton
Bedfordshire
LU10 9N

Builder's Address

A Builder
Head Office
The Drive
Saxon Estate
Newtown
Bucks
HP1 1XY

Order Reference: ABC

The separating walls and/or floors, listed below as applicable to this home, have been properly constructed in accordance with the relevant robust details specification sheets and associated checklist

Wall Robust Detail Type	Floor Robust Detail Type	Unique Reference
E-WM-4	E-FC-1	E13000562F

Signed...Print Name...

Position...

Representing   **A Builder**

Date..

Collating Certification & Commissioning

A Gas Safe Certificate will be issued by your plumber or heating engineer. If any appliances or fires are fitted individually and by a different contractor then they will also be required to issue you with a Gas Safe Certificate. It is vital to ensure any contractor you employ to install a gas supply is Gas Safe Registered.

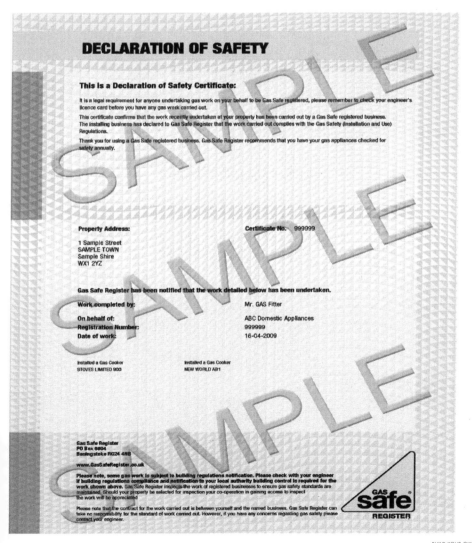

DECLARATION OF SAFETY

This is a Declaration of Safety Certificate:

It is a legal requirement for anyone undertaking gas work on your behalf to be Gas Safe registered, please remember to check your engineer's licence card before you have any gas work carried out.

This certificate confirms that the work recently undertaken at your property has been carried out by a Gas Safe registered business. The installing business has declared to Gas Safe Register that the work carried out complies with the Gas Safety (Installation and Use) Regulations.

Thank you for using a Gas Safe registered business. Gas Safe Register recommends that you have your gas appliances checked for safety annually.

Property Address:

1 Sample Street
SAMPLE TOWN
Sample Shire
WX1 2YZ

Certificate No.: 999999

Gas Safe Register has been notified that the work detailed below has been undertaken.

Work completed by: Mr. GAS Fitter

On behalf of: ABC Domestic Appliances

Registration Number: 999999

Date of work: 16-04-2009

Installed a Gas Cooker
STOVES LIMITED 900

Installed a Gas Cooker
NEW WORLD AB1

Gas Safe Register
PO Box 6804
Basingstoke RG24 4NB

www.GasSafeRegister.co.uk

Please note, some gas work is subject to building regulations notification. Please check with your engineer if building regulations compliance and notification to your local authority building control is required for the work shown above. Gas Safe Register inspects the work of registered businesses to ensure gas safety standards are maintained. Should your property be selected for inspection your co-operation in gaining access to inspect the work will be appreciated.

Please note that the contract for the work carried out is between yourself and the named business. Gas Safe Register can take no responsibility for the standard of work carried out. However, if you have any concerns regarding gas safety please contact your engineer.

GAS safe REGISTER

Structural Warranty Guarantee Certificate of Cover

Duty of Care Controlled Waste Transfer Note

(This is just an example of a transfer Note which you may use or adapt for your specific needs providing the same relevant information is contained)

Section A – Description of the Waste

Please describe the type of waste below: (e.g. "Plastic bale wrap)

Please give the six figure European Waste Catalogue Code (EWC code) for the waste below: (information on EWC codes can be found at http://europa.eu.int/eur-lex/en/consleg/pdf/2000/en_2000D0532_do_001.pdf)

Total quantity of waste to be collected: (e.g. number of sacks, weight)

Section B – Waste Producer (your name and address)

Name:

Address:

Postcode:

Telephone:

Email:

Signature:

Section C – Person or company Collecting the Waste

Name:

Address:

Postcode:

Telephone:

Email:

Name:

Signature on behalf of person or company collecting waste:

Which of the following is the person or company collecting the waste? (Please tick appropriate box)

Local Authority		
Holder of a waste management licence or permit	Licence or permit number: Issued by:	
Exempt from requirement to have a waste management licence or permit	Give reason: (e.g. exemption registration number)	
Registered waste carrier	Registration number:	
Exempt from requirement to register as a waste carrier	Give reason: (e.g. only carry agricultural waste)	

Section D

Address of place of transfer / collection point::

Date of transfer		Time of transfer	

Name and address of broker who arranged transfer (if applicable):

Structural Warranty cover will be critical for new build properties and will enable you to obtain a mortgage on your new property. Your Warranty provider will require all the above certification in place, where applicable, along with a copy of the Occupation Certificate, Planning Permission and Building Regulation approval. A Waste Transfer Note (WTN) is documentation that details the transfer of waste from one place to another, (WTN are not required for household waste). All waste material that needs removal from your site needs to be covered by a WTN. Waste Transfer Notes ensure there is a clear audit trail from where it is produced until it is disposed of. WTN must be kept for at least 2 years and may be required to be produced on demand to the Environment Agency or Local Council.

A Validation Certificate - This should accompany the delivery of imported soil or fill material that may be required. It proves that the imported material is fit for purpose. It is important that the original source of any material is known and in some instances validation of top soil or imported fill is a requirement of the **EHO (Environmental Health Organization)**. If fill or top soil has not been validated additional onsite testing maybe required.

COMMISSIONING

Commissioning is the process of making sure all the electrical and mechanical elements of your new dwelling are working satisfactorily prior to occupation. Commissioning should be carried out prior to occupation by the contractor who was responsible for the original installation.
The following are installations that will require commissioning:

- Heating and Hot Water System
- Fire and Smoke Detectors
- Alarm Systems
- Any sustainable systems such as Photo Voltaic, Solar Thermal, Rainwater Harvester and Ground Source heat pumps
- Home Entertainment systems

At the commissioning stage, you and any other occupants of your new dwelling should be present and shown how to operate all installations correctly.

MOVING IN

Moving in to your new home should be enjoyable with a real sense of achievement, and let's hope it is. In reality it's often a stressful experience. However with some good pre-planning you should be able to make your move an enjoyable experience.

If your budget allows try to have curtains, carpets and any other floor finishes that may be required fitted before you move in (it is far easier to have carpets laid in an empty house).

When arranging for carpets to be fitted enquire if the price for laying carpets includes having the bottoms of the doors trimmed. If not you will need to get your carpenter/joiner back to site after the carpets are laid to undertake this work.
Before your carpet fitter turns up ensure all floors are clean, flat and dry. For about 48 hours prior to and after installation, the temperature should stay between 180C and 350C and humidity between 20% and 65%. By observing these conditions your carpet installation should go smoothly.

If you are having curtains and blinds fitted try to have all poles and tracks put up before any carpets are laid. It is a good idea to have a folder where you can keep all relevant instructions together, such as heating controls and cooker instructions. If any new appliances have been purchased ensure all guarantees have been registered.

When moving out of a previous address ensure all meter readings have been taken and the utility companies have been informed.
Leave all instructions for heating systems and appliances ready for the new occupier. When booking your removal company contact numbers for reputable removers can be found at:
The British Association of Removers **(www.bar.co.uk)**

Changing Address -
Here is a Contacts Checklist

Financial Services

Subject	Contact Details	Notes	Done
Bank/Building Society			☐
Credit Card Companies			☐
Loans			☐
Hire Purchase Agreements			☐
Pensions & Investments			☐
Store Cards			☐

Insurance Providers

Subject	Contact Details	Notes	Done
Car			☐
Contents & Buildings			☐
Life			☐
Health/Medical			☐

Government Agencies

Subject	Contact Details	Notes	Done
Benefit Providers			☐
Council Tax Office - Old & New			☐
DVLA - Car Registration & Licence			☐
Electoral Commission			☐

Moving In

Utilities & Services

Subject	Contact Details	Notes	Done
Gas			☐
Electricity			☐
Water			☐
Phone/Mobile Phone Company			☐
Internet Service Provider			☐
Cable/Satellite Company			☐
TV Licensing			☐
Royal Mail - Mail Redirection			☐
Breakdown Services			☐

Health Providers

Subject	Contact Details	Notes	Done
Doctor/Dentist			☐
Optician			☐
Medical Consultants			☐
Vet			☐
Donor Card			☐

BUILD YOUR OWN
HOUSE

Moving In

Miscellaneous

Subject	Contact Details	Notes	Done
School/College/University			☐
Employer			☐
Loyalty Cards			☐
Gyms, Sport Clubs & Social Groups			☐
Milk/Other Deliveries			☐
Library			☐
Publications/Subscriptions			☐
Charities			☐
Trade Unions/Professional Bodies			☐
Video Rental			☐

Other

Subject	Contact Details	Notes	Done
			☐
			☐
			☐
			☐
			☐
			☐

HEALTH AND SAFETY

The construction industry is one of the most dangerous sectors in the United Kingdom and everyone involved in a project has a duty of care. When planning your project it is vital you understand the responsibility for which you are liable. Health and Safety has been put in place to reduce risk along with CDM (Construction Design and Management) Regulations 2007. These are legal requirements.

CDM 2007 Regulations are divided into 5 parts:

- Part 1 deals with the application of the regulations and definitions
- Part 2 covers general duties that apply to all construction projects
- Part 3 contains additional duties that only apply to notifiable construction projects, i.e. those lasting more than 30 days or involving more than 500 person days of construction work
- Part 4 contains practical requirements that apply to all construction sites
- Part 5 contains the transitional arrangements and revocations

CDM regulations do not apply to Self-Builders unless they are taking control over an aspect of a project. You will then have duties under Part 4 of the CDM regulations.

Part 4 includes duties relating to Health and Safety on Construction Sites and includes the following:

Safe places of work
Good order and site security
Stability of structures
Demolition or dismantling
Explosives
Excavations
Cofferdams and caissons
Reports of inspections
Energy distribution installations
Prevention of drowning
Traffic Routes

Health And Safety

Vehicles
Prevention of risk from fire etc
Emergency procedures
Emergency routes and exits
Fire detection and fire-fighting
Fresh air
Temperature and weather protection
Lighting

Contractors, designers and any other workers hired by a Self-Builder (client) will still have duties under the CDM regulations. Depending on your approach to your project, including what aspects of your project you will be involved with will affect which Health and Safety laws apply to you. The following sets out common self-build methods and how Health and Safety law may apply. If you are unsure whether Health and Safety law relates to your own specific project further guidance can be obtained by contacting the HSE:

www.hse.gov.uk

The Do-It-Yourself approach – If you decide to carry out all the work yourself Health and Safety legislation will not apply. However, it is still best to follow HSE guidelines to ensure your project is constructed in a safe manner.

Self-Managed projects – If you are intending to manage the overall project and are intending employing contractors to undertake specific tasks, Part 4 of CDM regulation will apply, as you are exercising control and managing the building work. Under the regulations you have a duty to ensure the work under your control is being carried out safely, hired contractors are competent, on-site risks are properly controlled and all people on site co-operate with each other.

Hiring a Principle Contractor – If you hire or appoint a principle contractor to manage and complete the entire project, then you may not be required to undertake any duties under CDM, but if you do assert control over any aspects of your project you will have duties under Part 4 of CDM.

Whether or not you have any duties yourself, you should ensure your contractor is following Health and Safety procedures and all records are being kept.

As a self-builder if you directly employ any workers the Health and Safety Act 1974 will apply.

The Act lays out general workplace health and safety principles for employers, employees and the self-employed to assess and reduce the severity of risks in the workplace as much is reasonable practicable. Employers must abide by all relevant Health and Safety regulations including the following:

- The Management of Health and Safety at Work Regulations 1999
- The Work at Heights Regulations 2005
- Reporting of Injuries, Diseases and Dangerous Occurrences Regulations 1995
- The Health and Safety (First Aid) Regulations 1981

Note !
Never take the 'it won't happen to me attitude'. Make sure you have the correct insurance cover in place.

Insurance – Ensure before any work starts on site you have the correct insurance in place. You need insurance to cover the following:
- Public Liability Insurance (usually £5 million of cover)
- Employers Liability Insurance (usually £10 million of cover)

Further cover if required:
- Contract Works Insurance – to cover the cost for your self –build while under construction
- Plant and tools owned by you
- Tools and personal effects owned by your employees

Anyone who has lent you money for your project, such as banks and building societies, may require you to take out insurance cover.

Health And Safety

Health And Safety Checklist

Managing:
● Give enough time to properly plan and organise your work
● Check what is happening on your site, stop any practices you consider dangerous
● If Health and Safety advice is required contact HSE's info line on 08701 545500
● Take pride in setting good standards

Reporting Accidents
● Accidents need to be reported if:
1 – The accident is fatal or involves major surgery such as a fracture or loss of sight
2 – Any accident results in more than three consecutive days off
3 – A member of the public is killed or sent to hospital as a result of an accident on your site

Accidents should be reported by telephoning 0845 300 9923, via the internet at www.riddor.gov.uk or in writing using the form in HSe31 (rev 1) and then either faxing it to 0845 300 9924 or posting to:

**Incident Contact Centre
Caerphilly Business Park
Caerphilly CF83 3GG**

The reporting should be done by an appointed person.

Employing people
● Ensure they are competent and trained to do the job safely without putting their or anybody else's health at risk
● Ensure they are supervised and given clear instructions
● Make them aware of any on-site health and safety issues
● Be aware you are responsible for people under your control
● Ensure correct PPE is worn

Tidy sites and decent welfare
● Keep the site tidy and all materials safely stored
● Provide clean toilets
● Provide running hot and cold water with soap and towels

BUILD YOUR OWN
HOUSE

Health And Safety

- Provide drinking water
- Provide a basin large enough to immerse your arms up to the elbows
- You will need to provide somewhere warm, dry and clean to sit and eat

Access on Site
- Make sure everyone can get to their place of work safely
- Keep all access routes in good condition
- Provide edge protection where people are in danger of falling
- Any holes should have barriers around them or be covered
- Ensure there is adequate lighting

Scaffolds
- Only allow suitably qualified and competent people to erect or adapt scaffolding
- Ensure all uprights are provided with base and sole plates
- Ensure there are double guard rails and toe boards or other suitable protection at every edge, to prevent falling
- Where materials are present ensure brick guards are in place
- Ensure there are warning notices in place to stop people using an incomplete scaffold
- Never overload a scaffold
- Have a competent person inspect the scaffold at least once a week and after any alterations have been made
- Check scaffolds for damage after extreme weather conditions
- Make sure inspections are recorded
- Make sure scaffold towers are erected and being used in accordance with the supplier's instructions

Ladders
- Make sure ladders are the right way up
- Ensure all ladders are in good condition
- Secure all ladders at the top to prevent them slipping sideways or outwards
- Ensure ladders are at least 1m above the height of the landing
- Ensure ladders are positioned at the correct angle, 1 in 4

Health And Safety

Roof work

- Ensure edge protection is in place to prevent people or materials falling
- Never work on roofs in bad weather
- Never throw down waste or equipment
- Keep people away from the area below the roof work

Excavations

- Make sure excavations are battered back to prevent collapse
- Use a safe method of putting in supports without people entering an un-supported trench
- Provide safe access into and out of all excavation
- Provide barriers to stop people and vehicles falling in
- Store all materials, spoil and plant away from the edges of all excavations to reduce the chance of a collapse
- Ensure excavations don't affect the stability of neighbouring structures or services
- Have a competent person inspect all excavations before every shift

Manual Handling

- Chose lighter materials where possible
- Use wheelbarrows, hoists, telehandlers or any other plant or equipment so that manual handling of heavy equipment can be kept to a minimum
- Train people how to lift safely
- Try to avoid repetitive handling

Traffic Vehicles and Plant

- Use barriers and warning signs to separate vehicles and people
- Create clearance around slewing vehicles
- Ensure all plant is well maintained and its operators are properly trained
- Don't use plant or vehicles on dangerous slopes
- Avoid reversing where at all possible
- Ensure all loads are properly secured
- Make sure passengers are only carried on vehicles that are designed to carry them.

BUILD YOUR OWN
HOUSE

Tools and Machinery
- Ensure the right tools are being used for the right job
- Make sure all guards are correctly fitted
- Ensure all tools and machinery are maintained in good repair and all safety devices are operating correctly
- Make sure all operators are trained and competent

Emergencies
- Ensure evacuation procedures are in place in case of fire
- Make sure you have adequate first aid conditions
- Provide adequate escape routes
- Ensure there is a way of contacting the emergency services

Fire
- Try and keep the quantity of flammable material to a minimum
- Ensure gas cylinders are returned to a ventilated store at the end of each shift
- Provide suitable fire extinguishers
- When gas cylinders are not in use make sure the valves are fully closed
- Ensure any flammable and combustible waste is removed regularly and stored in suitable bins or skips
- Ban smoking in areas where gas or flammable liquids are stored or used

Hazardous Substances
- Make sure all hazardous substances have been identified, such as asbestos, solvents, paints and cement
- Consider using a work method where hazardous substances won't be required
- Once hazardous substances have been identified ensure proper control measures are in place
- Workers should be informed and trained accordingly in the handling of any hazardous materials, to avoid any risk
- Try to reduce noise, using different working methods or selecting quieter plant, such as having breakers and other plant fitted with silencers
- Ensure suitable hearing protection is provided and worn in noisy areas

- Make workers aware of the risks of exposure to noise and what they need to do to avoid those risks
- Identify hearing protection zones

Electricity and Other Services
- Make sure all necessary services have been provided on site before work begins. All existing services on site should have been identified and effective steps taken to prevent danger from them, i.e. identifying the routes they take.
- Ensure all tools are low voltage and battery operated
- Protect all leads and cables
- All electric tools should be regularly inspected and tested by a competent person
- Where there are overhead lines turn off electricity if possible or take other precautions, such as providing goal posts or taped markers

Protecting the Public
- Use signage to indicate the dangers of a building site and that no un-authorised access is permitted
- Ensure work is fenced off from the public
- Ensure the public are protected from any falling materials
- At the end of every shift make the boundary secure, remove or board ladders so they cannot be used, immobilise plant, ensure all materials are safely stacked and make sure any flammable or dangerous substances are locked away in secure storage places.

SAFETY FIRST

RECLAIMING VAT

When constructing new dwellings elements of the construction have a zero VAT rating. HMRC have a refund scheme in place for self-builders enabling them to reclaim VAT paid on some of the materials and labour used in self-build projects.

Projects where VAT refund scheme applies
- The construction of a new dwelling where someone is intending to live
- The conversion of a non-residential building into a dwelling. This is defined by never been lived in or been unoccupied for the last 10 years.
- Completion of a partially-built dwelling that has not been previously occupied. The dwelling must be self-contained accommodation.
- The construction of a new dwelling on the site of a former property, providing the original structure has been completely demolished to ground level (you may retain any basements or cellars).
- The construction of a new dwelling incorporating a party wall of an existing property

Projects where VAT refund scheme does not apply
- If the new property has planning conditions preventing it being sold or used separately from another property
- A property not intended for your use or a relative's use, but to let out or use for other business purposes
- Work carried out on a completed house that has been purchased from a developer or builder such as: conservatories, patios, double glazing, tiling or adding a garage

Evidence
HMRC will require evidence that work has been completed on your new property. HMRC will accept the following as evidence that you property is finished:

- A certificate or letter from the local authority, for Building Regulations purposes
- A Habitation or Occupation Certificate
- A valuation rating or council tax assessment
- A letter from your bank or building society stating that the last instalment of its loan on the dwelling has been released and it is regarded as complete

A building is normally considered complete when it has been finished according to its original plans. Where there is any doubt it may regarded as still under construction until the date that the local building control authority issues you with a completion certificate.

Important: - You can make only one claim per dwelling and that claim can be made no later than 3 months after construction work has been completed.

Information that may be required by HMRC:

VAT FORM
If you have a completion certificate you should send a copy of it with your VAT claim form.

- Approved plans from Local Planning department
- Copies of external elevations
- Internal floor plans showing what rooms your property contains

Reclaiming VAT
You can only claim for building materials and cannot claim for services. HMRC will supply you with a schedule where all invoices should be listed, indicating the VAT content. To support your claim all original invoices should be sent, these should all be in your name. If this is not the case you must explain why. (You may be purchasing materials on someone else's account. If so make sure the delivery address is shown).

If you choose to show reclaimed VAT invoices on your own spreadsheet then it must match the HMRC format. When working out your claim you must subtract any credits or discounts given by a supplier, such as for returned goods or bulk purchases. Since 4 January 2011 the standard rate of VAT is charged at 20% but this figure can vary. If only the VAT inclusive amount has been shown on your invoice you will have to work out the VAT element.

Purchases abroad

You can claim back the VAT on building materials that have been bought in any member state of the EU. For the purposes of your claim you should convert the amount of VAT you have been charged to sterling. You can also claim back the VAT paid on importing building materials into the EU. When making your claim you must provide evidence of the VAT paid, together with any originals of any shipping or transit documents showing the importation of the goods from abroad.

VAT invoice must show the following information:
- The price of each item
- Your name and address if the value is more than £100
- The quantity and description of the goods and/or services
- The suppliers VAT registration number must be on the invoice

The time period to obtain a refund

This is within 5 days of receiving your claims form. The HMRC should send you an acknowledgment, which will have a claims reference number. You will need this if any further correspondence is required.

HMRC aim to deal with all claims within six weeks unless more information is required. If your claim is successful you will be written to and informed when you can expect your refund from the National Payment Centre.

Building Materials you can claim for must meet the following conditions:

1- Articles claimed for must be incorporated into the building during construction

2 - Other than kitchen furniture no other item should be prefabricated

3 - The articles are not carpet or made from a carpeting material

4 - All articles should be fixed and require tools to remove them or result in either the need for remedial work to the fabric of the building or cause substantial damage to the goods themselves

Reclaiming VAT

Listed are goods you cannot claim for:

- Range cookers (unless they have been designed to be part of the hot water and/or heating system
- Garden furniture, garden ornaments and sheds
- Curtains, blinds and carpets
- Bedroom furniture
- Bathroom furniture such as vanity units and mirrors
- Electrical components for garage doors and gates (including remote controls)
- Consumables such as sandpaper, masking tape and white spirit
- Audio equipment including speakers, intelligent lighting systems, satellite boxes, CCTV and telephones
- Free-standing and integrated appliances such as: cookers, fridges, freezers, dishwashers, microwaves, washing machines, dryers and coffee machines

Goods that you can claim for:

The list would be too vast to incorporate all goods, but this list should give an idea of what is allowed:

- Air conditioning
- Bathroom accessories such as fixed towel rails, toilet roll holders, soap dishes, etc
- Building materials that make up the fabric of the building such as bricks, blocks, tiles, cement timber etc
- Burglar alarms
- Curtain rails and poles
- Decorating materials
- Doors and windows
- Dust extractors and filters including built-in vacuum cleaners
- Fencing that is permanently fixed around the boundary of the dwelling
- Fire places and their surrounds
- Fire alarms
- Fitted kitchen furniture
- Floor materials (other than carpets and carpet tiles)

- Gas and electrical appliances when wired or plumbed in are designed to provide ventilation, air cooling or purification or dust extraction
- Guttering
- Heating systems including radiators, controls, underfloor heating, ducted warm air systems, storage heaters and other wired-in heating appliances.
- Immersion heaters, boilers, hot and cold water tanks.
- Kitchen sinks, work surfaces and fitted cupboards
- Letter boxes
- Lifts and hoists
- Light fittings, chandeliers and outside lights
- Saunas / Shower units
- Smoke detectors
- Solar panels
- Turf, plants and trees (that are detailed as part of planning permission)
- TV aerials and satellite dishes
- Ventilation equipment such as cooker hoods
- Wiring (including power and computer circuits, phone and TV cabling)

You can check items that can be claimed for here: HMRC **0845 010 9000**

Checklist (ensure the following documents are also provided)

- A copy of the Planning approval
- Evidence the construction work is complete
- Plans, floor plans, elevations and any landscaping details that were required as part of the planning approval
- All the original VAT invoices, bills and credit notes

Send completed forms and documents to:
Local Compliance
National DIY Team S0987
PO Box 3900
Glasgow
G70 6AA

BUILD YOUR OWN
HOUSE

visit
www.buildyourownhouse.biz
for more information about self-builds, build your own house
UK seminars with Andy Patmore and much more.

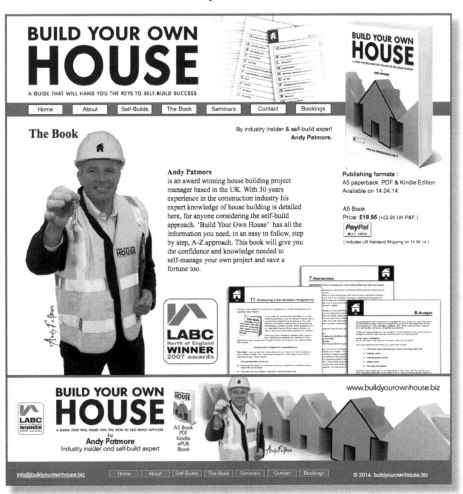

Email: **info@buildyourownhouse.biz**

A

acoustic test certificate,192
air leakage,42
air permeability test ,188
air permeability test certificate,189
air permeability test report,187
air pressure testing,162
air tightness,42
air tightness testing,161
airborne sound,161
airborne testing,160
alternative foundation,77
appeals,18
appliances,
approval notice,17
approved documents,36
approved plans,17
architect certificate,43
architects practice,14
Architectural Practice,11
architraves,133

B

balustrades,132
basements,100
beam and block,92,93
bill of quantities,24,25
biomass boilers,39
block and render,95,97
block paving,147
BLP (building life plan),43
boundary walls,150
BRE (Building Research Establishment),90
BRE certification Ltd,121
brick and block,95,96
brick built manhole,87
brick finish timber framed wall,99
bricks and blocks,91
brickwork gables,167
brickwork to DPC,164
brickwork to joist,166
British Association of Removers (BAR),196
British Geological Survey,71
BSI,121
BT connection,58
BT Land line,59
budget,10,132
build ability,48
build clean,144
build costs,46,48
building leakage test,190,191
building near trees,70,73
building regulation approval,30

building regulation compliance,181
building regulation drawings,30
building regulations,36,80,122
building water charge,55

C

CAD designer,14
CAD technician,47
carports,149
case driven piles,78
case officer,16,17
cavity fill,159
cavity insulation,129
CDM,124,
CDM 2007 Regulations,200
changing address,196
check list,64,212
clay board,74
clay roof tiles,113
cleaning,174
code for sustainable homes ,37,38,184,185,186
code of practice for painting of buildings,141
combed wheat reed,114
commissioning,195
concrete roof tiles,113
conservation approval,61
conservation of fuel and power,36
conservatories,152
construction costs,22
construction programme ,11,64,66
construction programme considerations,64
contaminated area,73
contaminated ground,90
contaminated land,34,35
contractor (hiring a principle contractor),201
control of substances hazardous to health,63
correct insulation,94
correct mortar,91
COSHH,63
cost specification,24
Council of Mortgage Lenders (CML),45
coursed stone,95,98
covenants,21
cover for flexible drainage pipes,87
cover for rigid drainage pipes,87
cut perlin roof,109

D

damp proof course (DPC),33,36
decking,167
decorating structural steel,142
decoration,173

delays,65
design and access statement,15
design costs,46
design for cleaning safely,124
design of your new home,61
design technicians,22
detailed investigation,72,73
disabled access,36,67,119
Distribution Network Operator (DNO),55,56
distributors,55
domestic building service compliance guide,137
domestic hot water system
doors,23
downspouts,168
DPC (Damp Proof Course),89,94,90
DPM (Damp proof Membrane,90,91
drainage,20,31,165
drainage and waste disposal,36
drainage design,79
drained area,83
drive ways,145,146
driven piles,78
dry lining,130,171
ducting,57

E
eaves detail,107
EHO (Environmental Health Organisation),195
electric,50
electric meters,155
electrical safety,36
electrical test certificate,34
electricity,55
electricity and other services,207
electrics,138
elevations,15
emergencies,206
emergency services,68
employing people,203
enabling works,22,67
energy performance certificate (EPC),34,37,42,177
engineers,69
Environment Agency,71
EPC (energy performance certificate),176
excavating,52
Excavations,57,205
external decoration,168
external doors,169
external doors and windows,120
external render,130,168
external wall construction,95
external works,24,174

extras,12

F
fences,150
fencing,67
FFL (finished floor level),69
final fix,143
finance,26,27,46,49
finishing and decorative materials,60
fink truss roof,106
fire precautions,36
fire resistance,128,206
first fix,169
first fix electrics,170
first fix plumbing,117,170
first floor plan,12
first lift brickwork,165
first lift scaffold,166
flat roof,110
floor and wall tiling,137
floor construction,91
floor joists,102,103,201,101,167
floor slab,33
foul water,32,79
foul water drainage,79
foundations,23,32,70,75,76,88,164
front elevation,19
frost,76
full fill cavity wall,97

G
garages,129,149,175
gas,50,53
gas meter position,51
gas meters,154
gas safe certificate,34,193
gas safety regulations,52
general building materials,60
geotechnical investigation,72
generators,55
glazing,38,127
government publications,38
gravel,147
green deal scheme,42
ground conditions,70,71,73
ground description,72
ground floor slab,165
ground source heat pumps,38
guttering,168

H
hand cut roofs,109

Index

handrails,132
hazardous substances,206
Health and Safety,200
hearing,18
heating appliances,36
heating controls,38,39
heating systems,38,94,136
HMRC,208,209
hot water system,136
hygiene,36

I

ICF (insulated concrete formwork),95,100
incoming services,50,90
incoming water,83
independent wall,159
infrastructure,20
infrastructure costs,46,47
installation,124
installing underground drainage,86
insulated plasterboard,129
insulation,38
insurance,202
internal doors,134
internal plastering,130
internal walls,95,118

J

Japanese knotweed,35
joists,33

K

key stage inspections,31
kitchen,134,171

L

LABC,31,44
LABC warranty,43
ladders,204
land registry documents,29
landscaping,153
legal fees,46
lighting,139
lintels,101
local authority building control (LABC),30
local authority planning department,61
Local Compliance,212
local historic records and government offices,71
local planning authority (LPA),16
Location,9
loft insulation,143

long straw,114

M

maintenance,124
manhole construction,86
manual handling,205
mastic pointing,144
material change,18
material schedule,61,62
max pitch,116
MCS accredited installer,39
media,50,58,157
meter box locations,52
meters,58
methodology of designing foundations,58,70
mono-pitch roof,111
mortar,91
mortgage,27,29
moving in,196
MPAN (meter point administration number),58,155
multi layered foil insulation,129

N

National Coal Board,71
National Grid,51,53
neighbours,68
NHBC (National House Build Council),43,44,163
NICEIC,121
noggins,119
noise,160
non material change,18

O

occupation certificate,176,12
OFGEN,156
ordnance survey,69,71
outbuildings,150
outflow volume,83
oversite slab,23

P

panelised roofing system,109
parge coating,129,159
partial fill cavity wall,96
paths,148
percolation test,81
percolation test calculations,85
percolation test method,82
permeability test,32
photovoltaic panels,39
pile detail,78

piled foundation,78
pipes passing through wall,89
planning,14,15,122
planning amendments,17
planning committee,17
planning consultants,14,21
planning consultation,15
planning fees,16,21
planning permission,21
plastering,171
plot search,10
pointing,120
polyethylene,54
position of internal drains,89
position of water table,80,81
positioning of a soakaway,80,83
premier guarantee,43
pre-plaster inspection,120
prim cost,25,48
procurement,49
professional indemnity insurance,43
Project Manager,10,11
protecting the public,207

Q
Quantity Surveyor,11,25
quilt insulation,129

R
raft foundation,77
rainwater harvesting,40,41
rear elevation,19
reclaiming VAT,208,209
refund scheme,208
reinforcing,77
remediation techniques,73
render,159
render below DPC,97
rendered timber framed wall,99
reporting accidents,203
retaining walls,151
reverberation times,160
robust details,159,192
roof construction,106,167
roof coverings,23,111,168
roof truss,108
roof work,204
rooflights,125
roofs,23,33,110

S
sanitary ware,140

SAP (standard assessment procedure),176
SAP rating,33
scaffolding,97,104,105,169
scaffolds,169,204
screw and plug,124
sealant,174
second fix electrics,138,173
second fix joinery,171
second fix plumbing,172
security,124
self-build,9
self-build mortgage,29
self-build zone,43
self-managed projects,201
services,20,50,59
setting out,69
sewage treatment,83
sheds,150
side elevation,19
signage,67
SIPS (structural insulated panels),95,100
site layout,13
site location plan,12
site parking,67
site plan,15,68
site preparation,164
site purchase,20,46
site remediation,73
skirting boards,133
slate roofs,112
smart meter,154,155
soakaway,32,81
soakaway drains,86
soil survey maps,71
solar thermal,39,40
sound insulation,128,129
sound resistance between dwellings,36
sound testing,158
structural engineers,70
stairs,115,116
stairways,36
start date ,64
steelwork,101
stepped foundation,76
stone face,98
stone vibrio piles,78
straps,124
strip foundation,75
structural guarantee,44
structural stability,36
structural warranty,29,43,45
structural warranty guarantee,194
structural evidence,72

Index

substructure,89
superstructure,23,95
suppliers,55
surface and ground water,72
surface water,32,79
surface water drainage,79,80
surface water soakaway design,80
swimming pools,153

T
tarmacadam,147
TBM (temporary bench mark),69
telephones,156
temporary roads,67
temporary services,68
test failure,161
thatched roof,114
thermal insulation,128
threshold detail,148
timber decking,152
timber fences,151
timber frame,95,98
timber frame kits,98
timber kit,98
timber suspended floor,93
time scales,65
toilet and washing facilities,68
tools and machinery,205
topography,71
toxic substances,36
TRADA,102
traffic vehicles and plant,205
trees and vegetation,72
trench foundations,74,76
truss manufactures,108
trussed roofs,106

U
Ukradon,90
utilities,47,59,134
U-values,96

V
validation,35
validation certificate,195
VAT,208
VAT form,209
VAT invoices,210
ventilation of habitable rooms and unheated voids,36
viability assessment,26
visibility splay,145

W
wall abutment,110
wall and floor tiling,172
wall construction,33
wall plate,167
wall ties,104
walling stone,95
warranty,43
water,50,53,54
water meters,154
water reed,114
water test,88
water treatment plant,84
way leaves,20
wet wall boards,138
WIAPS certificate,54
wind turbines,39
window and door openings,104
window boards,120
window head and lintel,101
window reveal,125
windows,23,36,169
wiring,121
working at height regulations 2005,105

Z
Zurich Ltd,121